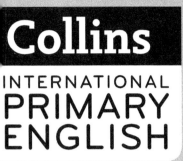

Collins

INTERNATIONAL PRIMARY ENGLISH

Teacher's Guide 2

William Collins' dream of knowledge for all began with the publication of his first book in 1819. A self-educated mill worker, he not only enriched millions of lives, but also founded a flourishing publishing house. Today, staying true to this spirit, Collins books are packed with inspiration, innovation and practical expertise. They place you at the centre of a world of possibility and give you exactly what you need to explore it.

Collins. Freedom to teach.

An imprint of HarperCollins*Publishers*
The News Building
1 London Bridge Street
London SE1 9GF

Browse the complete Collins catalogue at
www.collins.co.uk

10 9 8 7 6 5 4 3 2

ISBN 978-0-00-814765-5

Joyce Vallar asserts her moral rights to be identified as the author of this work.

British Library Cataloguing in Publication Data
A catalogue record for this publication is available from the British Library.

Publisher Celia Wigley
Publishing manager Karen Jamieson
Commissioning editor Lucy Cooper
Series editor Karen Morrison
Managing editor Caroline Green
Editor Amanda Redstone
Project managed by Emily Hooton and Karen Williams
Edited by Karen Williams
Proofread by Gaynor Spry
Cover design by Amparo Barrera
Cover artwork by David Roberts
Internal design by Ken Vail Graphic Design
Typesetting by Ken Vail Graphic Design and Contentra Technologies India Private Limited
Illustrations by Ken Vail Graphic Design, Advocate Art and Beehive Illustration
Production by Robin Forrester

Printed and bound by CPI Group (UK) Ltd, Croydon, CR0 4YY

Contents

Section 1 Introduction

Section 2 Unit-by-Unit Support

Unit 1: Fun and games

Unit 2: The Olympics

Unit 3: What's for lunch?

Unit 4: Kind Emma

Introduction

About Collins International Primary English

Collins Primary International English is specifically written to meet fully the requirements of the Cambridge International Examinations Primary English Framework, and the material has been carefully developed to meet the needs of primary English learners and teachers in a range of international contexts.

The material at each level has been organised into nine units, each based around particular text types. The activities in each unit are introduced and explored in contexts related to the selected texts.

The course materials are supplemented and enhanced by a range of print and electronic resources, including photocopiable (printable) master sheets for support, extension and assessment of classroom based activities (you can find these on pages 94 to 123 of this Teacher's Guide as well as on the digital resource) and a range of interactive digital activities to add interest and excitement to learning. Reading texts are supported by audio-visual presentations.

Components of the course

For each of Stages 1–6 as detailed in the Cambridge Primary English Framework, we offer:

- a full colour, highly illustrated Student's Book with integral reading texts
- a write-in Workbook linked to the Student's Book
- this comprehensive Teacher's Guide with clear instructions for using the materials
- an interactive digital package, which includes warm-up presentations, audio files of readings, interactive activities and record keeping for teacher use only.

Approach

The course is designed with learner-centred learning at its heart. Learners work through a range of contextualised reading, writing, speaking and listening activities with guidance and support from their teacher. Plenty of opportunity is provided for the learners to consolidate and apply what they have learnt and to relate what they are learning both to other contexts and the environment in which they live.

Much of the learners' work is conducted in pairs or small groups in line with international best practice. The tasks and activities are designed to be engaging for the learners and to support teachers in their assessment of learner progress and achievement. Each set of lessons is planned to support clear learning objectives and the activities within each unit provide opportunities for oral and written feedback by the teacher as well as self- and peer-assessment options.

Throughout the course, there is a wide variety of learning experiences on offer. The materials are organised so that they do not impose a rigid structure, but rather allow for a range of options linked to the learning objectives.

Differentiation

Differentiation in the form of support and extension ideas is built into the unit-by-unit teaching support in this Teacher's Book.

Achievement levels are likely to vary from learner to learner, so we have included a graded set of assessment criteria in each weekly review section. The square, circle and triangle assessment criteria indicate what learners at varying levels might be expected to have achieved each week. The square indicates what can be expected of almost all learners. The circle indicates what might be expected of most learners, and the triangle indicates what level of achievement might be expected from more able learners. Levels will vary as some learners may find some topics more interesting and/or easier; similarly, some may excel at speaking activities rather than written ones.

Teacher's Guide

The Teacher's Guide offers detailed guidance for covering each unit. Each unit is designed to cover three teaching weeks. The teacher knows their class and context best, so they should feel free to vary the pace and the amount of work covered each week to suit their circumstances. Each unit has a clear structure, with an introduction, suggestions for introducing the unit, learning objectives and a resource list of supporting materials that can be used in the unit.

Student's Book

The Student's Book offers a clear structure and easy-to-follow design to help learners to navigate the course. The following features are found at all levels:

- A range of fiction, non-fiction, poetry, play scripts and transactional texts are provided to use as a starting point for contextualised learning.
- Skills-based headers allow teachers to locate activities within the curriculum framework and indicate to learners what skills are being focussed on in each task.
- Clear instruction rubrics are provided for each activity. The rubrics allow learners to develop more and more independent learning as they begin to master and understand instructive text. The rubrics also model assessment type tasks and prepare them for formal assessment at all levels.
- Icons indicate where there is an audio-visual support for the text. Teachers can play these to the class and learners can use these themselves if they need to listen to the text again.
- Grammar and language boxes provide teaching text and examples to show the language feature in use. These are colour coded so that learners can easily recognise them as they work through the course.
- The notepad feature contains reminders, hints and interesting facts.

Workbook

The Workbook is clearly linked to the Student's Book. The activities here contain structured spaces for the learners to record answers. The activities can be used as classroom tasks, for homework, or for assessment purposes. The completed Workbook tasks give the teacher an opportunity to check work and give written feedback and/or grades. The learners have a consolidated record of their work and parents can see what kind of activities the learners are doing in class.

Digital resources

The digital resources are offered online by subscription. You can access these at Collins Connect. These resources can be used to introduce topics and support learning and assessment. The unit guidelines in this Teacher's Guide offer suggestions for when and how to use these resources.

The interactive activities include:

- drag-and-drop activities
- matching activities
- look-cover-say-spell activities
- cloze procedure (fill in the missing words)
- labelling diagrams
- and many more.

Learners receive instant feedback when they complete the activities and the responses are randomised so the learners can complete the tasks they enjoy more than once, getting a different arrangement of items each time.

Some materials can be printed out for use in the classroom. For example, there is an additional assessment task provided for each unit. This is in the form of a simple test. It can be printed and used in class or as a homework task. These tasks are teacher marked. There is also a set of activity sheets which can be used for support, extension and homework as required.

Collins Connect offers an easy and accessible method of keeping records. Teachers can compile class lists and keep track of progress in an easy-to-use and well-supported system.

Assessment in primary English

In the primary English programme, assessment is a continuous, planned process that involves collecting information about learner progress and learning in order to provide constructive feedback to both learners and parents and also to guide planning and the next teaching steps.

Cambridge International Examinations Primary English Curriculum Framework makes it clear what the learners are expected to learn and achieve at each level. Our task as teachers is to assess whether or not the learners have achieved the stated goals using clearly-focussed, varied, reliable and flexible methods of assessment.

In the Collins Primary English course, assessment is continuous and in-built. It applies the principles of international best practice and ensures that assessment:

- is ongoing and regular
- supports individual achievement and allows for learners to reflect on their learning and set targets for themselves
- provides feedback and encouragement to the learners
- allows for integration of assessment into the activities and classroom teaching by combining different assessment methods,

including observations, questioning, self-assessment and formal and informal tasks/tests

- uses strategies that cater for a variety of learner needs in the classroom (language, physical, emotional and cultural), and acknowledges that the learners do not all need to be assessed at the same time, or in the same way
- allows for, and prepares learners for, more formal summative assessment including controlled activities, tasks and tests.

Formal written assessment

The Collins International Primary English course offers a set of assessment sheets that teachers can use to assess learning formally and to award marks if necessary. These sheets test the skills and competencies developed in a cumulative manner. In some cases, learners will use the same texts as context, in other cases; they will be expected to read and make sense of an unseen text and to answer a range of contextualised questions based on that. At Stage 2, there is a short assessment task at the end of each unit.

In addition to the materials supplied in the course, schools may opt for their learners to take standardised Cambridge International progression tests at Stages 3, 4, 5 and 6. These tests are developed by Cambridge but they are written and marked in schools. Teachers download tests and administer them in their own classrooms. Cambridge International Examinations provides a mark scheme and you can upload learners' test results and then analyse the results and print reports. You can also compare a learner's results against their class, school or other schools around the world and on a year-by-year basis.

Laying the foundations of learning to read in the early stages

To learn to read and write, learners need to be phonologically aware and have a functional understanding of the alphabet along with an understanding of the purpose and value of print. Successful reading and writing depends on their ability to make the association between all three of these skills.

Learning to read should be treated as an enjoyable problem-solving activity. Learners must be encouraged to use a wide range of strategies to help them to read unknown words.

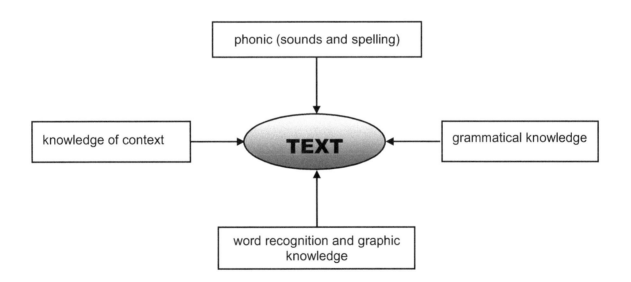

First 100 high frequency words

the	and	a	to	said
that	with	all	we	can
are	up	had	my	her
what	there	out	this	have
went	be	like	some	so
in	he	I	of	it
was	you	they	on	she
is	for	at	his	but
find	more	I'll	round	tree
magic	shouted	us	other	food
fox	through	way	been	stop
must	red	door	right	sea
these	began	boy	animals	never
next	first	work	lots	need
that's	baby	fish	gave	mouse
something	bed	may	still	found
live	say	soon	night	narrator
small	car	couldn't	three	head
king	town	I've	around	every
garden	fast	only	many	laughed

Phonics

Phonics is a strategy for teaching reading and spelling of the English language. It focuses on developing the learners' ability to hear, identify and manipulate phonemes, in order to teach the correspondence between these sounds and the spelling patterns that represent them. A phonics programme should foster a steady development of phonological and phonemic awareness.

Phonological awareness is an explicit awareness of the sounds in words, demonstrated by the ability to identify onset, generate rhyme and segment syllables in words.

The smallest unit of sound in a word is called a phoneme. There are approximately 44 phonemes in the English language. A phoneme can be formed by one, two, three or four letters. For example:

c as in 'cot' – one letter
ch as in 'chat' – two letters

–igh as in 'high' – three letters
–tion as in 'station' – four letters

'Cat' has three phonemes (*c-a-t*), but 'chat' also has three phonemes (*ch-a-t*).

The 44 sounds are represented by the 26 letters (graphemes) of the alphabet.

There are a number of skills that should be taught and practised in a phonic programme.

1 Letter sounds (phonemes)

Learning the letter sounds should include alphabet sounds as well as two letters making one sound, like *sh*, *ch*, *ng*. It should also include learning that the same sound can be represented in more than one way, such as *ai/ay* representing the long vowel *a* and the same spelling can represent more than one sound, such as *ow* in 'now' and 'show'.

2 Letter formation

Learners should learn to form the letters correctly and consistently.

3 Blending

Learners should learn to blend sounds together to read a word. In order to read an unfamiliar word phonemically a learner must attribute a phoneme (sound) to each letter or letter combination in the word and then merge the phonemes together to pronounce the word.

4 Segmenting

Learners should learn to listen and break a word down into its component sounds, for example, *c-a-t*, *sh-o-p*. Learners need to be able to do this to produce a written word (spelling) from a spoken word.

5 Onset and rime

Onset is the initial consonant or consonant cluster of letters (adjacent consonants) in words which precedes the vowel, for example '*b*ag', '*cl*ock'.

Rime refers to the vowel and final consonant(s). For example *–at* in 'cat', *–ing* in 'string' or the final digraph e.g. *–ow* in 'how', 'now', 'cow'.

When a learner is learning to read and write there are two crucial things to learn:

- the sounds represented by written letters.
- how to blend the sounds together to make a word, and how to break a word into its component sounds (segment) to spell a word.

Alphabet sounds – Learners should be given opportunities to learn the relationship between letter (grapheme) and sound (phoneme) and to hear, read and write the alphabet sounds. At first the focus is on the sound that an alphabet letter represents but the learners should learn the names of each alphabet letter and the sound each represents. You should use the words 'name' and 'sound' correctly when speaking to the learners. It is very important when teaching learners to learn the alphabet sounds, to remember not to add an *uh* to the end of consonant sounds – so say *mmm* and not *muh*. It is then easier to blend the sounds together to make words. The focus in the beginning is on letters as initial sounds as in '*h*at' and '*p*at', but very quickly every opportunity must be taken to make learners aware that sounds appear at the end of words as in 'ha*t*' and 'ha*d*', and in the middle of words as in 'h*a*t' and 'h*o*t'.

When learners have been taught a group of sounds they can then learn to blend the sounds to read words made up from those sounds. They can then be taught more sounds and learn to blend those too.

The order in which the sounds are taught will vary depending on which scheme is used in your school, but it shouldn't be alphabetical order as that is not the best order to allow learners to start blending the sounds for reading.

Some sounds are represented by more than one letter such as *sh* in 'ship', *ch* in 'chat'.

The powerful reason for looking at alphabet letters as sounds is to give learners a tool to read words and they must be encouraged to do so at all times. It is important for learners to know the sounds. It is more important for them to use the sounds as a reading strategy.

Concept of rhyme – Learners should also be given the opportunity to develop the concept of rhyme. They should have plenty of opportunities to become familiar with rhymes through listening to, joining in with and reciting and performing rhymes. When learners experience singing, chanting and learning rhymes they gradually develop a script for building rhyming skills through imitation and experimenting.

The three elements of rhyme are:

- an awareness of rhyme
- the ability to recognise and identify rhyme
- the ability to generate rhyme.

Segmenting and blending – Learners should be given every opportunity to develop an appreciation of blending individual sounds to make words, e.g. *c-a-t*/'cat', *sh-o-p*/'shop' and *b-oa-t*/'boat', and segmenting words into sounds, e.g. 'cat'/*c-a-t*, 'shop'/*sh-o-p* and 'boat'/*b-oa-t*.

They should be given opportunities to build words with letters using their sense of analogy and to see the resemblance between certain words. They should be given opportunities to read new words by changing the initial sound (onset) and by using the rime from the original word. For example:

hat	best	hop	boat
bat	nest	top	coat
fat	pest	shop	moat
sat	rest	chop	float

At the early stages every day should include some phonic activity. This may be in the form of direct teaching, reading lists of regular words, writing regular words (or using magnetic letters to form words) phonic games and activities or recapping/highlighting a phonic skill that arises from a text. You should take every opportunity to reinforce the learners learning by asking about/commenting on phonic skills recently taught.

Learning objectives matching grid

The types of reading texts and the objectives covered in each unit are listed here by strand for easy reference. These same objectives are listed at the beginning of each unit in the unit-by-unit *support* section of this book.

Unit 1	Reading	Writing	Listening and speaking
Fun and games Texts: *Jodie the Juggler* (story with a familiar setting) *Janet the Juggler* poem with alliteration and rhyme) *Sounds* (poem with onomatopoeic language)	2R01 Learn the different ways in which vowels can be pronounced, e.g. 'how', 'low'; 'apple', 'apron'; 2R02 Use phonics as the main method of tackling unfamiliar words; 2R03 Identify syllables and split familiar compound words into parts; 2R06 Read aloud with increased accuracy, fluency and expression; 2R07 Begin to read with fluency and expression, taking some notice of punctuation, including speech marks; 2R10 Discuss the meaning of unfamiliar words encountered in reading; 2Rx3 Find answers to questions by reading a section of text; 2Ri1 Predict story endings; 2Ri3 Make simple inferences from the words on the page, e.g. about feelings; 2Rw1 Comment on some vocabulary choices, e.g. adjectives; 2Rw2 Talk about what happens at the beginning, in the middle or at the end of a story; 2Rw3 Read poems and comment on words and sounds, rhyme and rhythm.	2W03 Begin to reread own writing aloud to check for sense and accuracy; 2W04 Use simple non-fiction texts as a model for writing; 2W05 Use the structures of familiar poems and stories in developing own writing; 2W07 Make simple notes from a selection of non-fiction texts, e.g. listing key words; 2Wa2 Choose interesting words and phrases, e.g. in describing people and places; 2Wa3 Build and use collections of interesting and significant words; 2Wa5 Use features of chosen text type; 2Wt1 Structure a story with a beginning, middle and end; 2Wt3 Link ideas in sections, grouped by content; 2Wp1 Write in clear sentences using capital letters, full stops and question marks; 2Ws1 Learn the different common spellings of long vowel phonemes; 2Ws2 Apply knowledge of phonemes and spelling patterns in writing independently as well as when writing sentences from memory dictated by the teacher.	2SL1 Recount experiences and explore possibilities; 2SL3 Articulate clearly so that others can hear; 2SL6 Attempt to express ideas precisely, using a growing vocabulary; 2SL8 Demonstrate 'attentive listening' and engage with another speaker; 2SL9 Extend experiences and ideas through role play; 2SL11 Show awareness that speakers use a variety of ways of speaking in different situations and try out different ways of speaking.

Unit 2	Reading	Writing	Listening and speaking
The Olympics Texts: *The Olympic Games* (non-fiction text)	2R02 Use phonics as the main method of tackling unfamiliar words; 2R04 Extend the range of common words recognised on sight; 2R06 Read aloud with increased accuracy, fluency and expression; 2R07 Begin to read with fluency and expression, taking some notice of punctuation, including speech marks; 2R08 Explore a variety of non-fiction texts on screen; 2R09 Locate words by initial letter in simple dictionaries, glossaries and indexes; 2R10 Discuss the meaning of unfamiliar words encountered in reading; 2Rx2 Read and follow simple instructions, e.g. in a recipe; 2Rx3 Find answers to questions by reading a section of text; 2Rx4 Find factual information from different formats, e.g. charts, labelled diagrams; 2Rv1 Show some awareness that texts have different purposes; 2Rv2 Identify general features of known text types.	2W04 Use simple non-fiction texts as a model for writing; 2W07 Make simple notes from a selection of non-fiction texts, e.g. listing key words; 2Wa2 Choose interesting words and phrases, e.g. in describing people and places; 2Wa3 Build and use collections of interesting and significant words; 2Wa5 Use features of chosen text type; 2Wt1 Structure a story with a beginning, middle and end; 2Wt4 Use a variety of simple organisational devices in non-fiction, e.g. headings, captions; 2Wp1 Write in clear sentences using capital letters, full stops and question marks; 2Ws1 Learn the different common spellings of long vowel phonemes; 2Ws2 Apply knowledge of phonemes and spelling patterns in writing independently as well as when writing sentences from memory dictated by the teacher 2Ws3 Secure the spelling of high frequency words and common irregular words.	2SL1 Recount experiences and explore possibilities; 2SL8 Demonstrate 'attentive listening' and engage with another speaker; 2SL6 Attempt to express ideas precisely, using a growing vocabulary.

Unit 3	Reading	Writing	Listening and speaking
What's for lunch? Texts: *Worm Looks for Lunch* (playscript) *Caterpillar* *The Caterpillar* (short rhyming poems by established poets for comparison)	2R02 Use phonics as the main method of tackling unfamiliar words; 2R06 Read aloud with increased accuracy, fluency and expression; 2R07 Begin to read with fluency and expression, taking some notice of punctuation, including speech marks; 2Ri2 Identify and describe story settings and characters, recognising that they may be from different times and places; 2R10 Discuss the meaning of unfamiliar words encountered in reading; 2Rx3 Find answers to questions by reading a section of text; 2Ri3 Make simple inferences from the words on the page, e.g. about feelings; 2R09 Locate words by initial letter in simple dictionaries, glossaries and indexes; 2Rv1 Show some awareness that texts have different purposes.	2W04 Use simple non-fiction texts as a model for writing; 2W07 Make simple notes from a selection of non-fiction texts, e.g. listing key words; 2Wa2 Choose interesting words and phrases, e.g. in describing people and places; 2Wa3 Build and use collections of interesting and significant words; 2Wp1 Write in clear sentences using capital letters, full stops and question marks; 2Wa5 Use features of chosen text type; 2Wt1 Structure a story with a beginning, middle and end; 2Wt2 Use the language of time, e.g. 'suddenly', 'after that'; 2Wp3 Use mainly simple and compound sentences, with and/but to connect ideas. Because may begin to be used in a complex sentence; 2Ws1 Learn the different common spellings of long vowel phonemes; 2Ws2 Apply knowledge of phonemes and spelling patterns in writing independently as well as when writing sentences from memory dictated by the teacher; 2Ws3 Secure the spelling of high frequency words and common irregular words.	2SL5 Show awareness of the listener by including relevant details; 2SL6 Attempt to express ideas precisely, using a growing vocabulary; 2SL8 Demonstrate 'attentive listening' and engage with another speaker; 2SL10 Begin to be aware of ways in which speakers vary talk, e.g. the use of more formal vocabulary and tone of voice; 2SL11 Show awareness that speakers use a variety of ways of speaking in different situations and try out different ways of speaking.

Unit 4	Reading	Writing	Listening and speaking
Kind Emma Texts: *Kind Emma* (traditional tale)	2R06 Read aloud with increased accuracy, fluency and expression; 2R07 Begin to read with fluency and expression, taking some notice of punctuation, including speech marks; 2R10 Discuss the meaning of unfamiliar words encountered in reading; 2Rx1 Read and respond to question words, e.g. 'what', 'where', 'when', 'who', 'why'; 2Rx3 Find answers to questions by reading a section of text; 2Ri1 Predict story endings; 2Ri2 Identify and describe story settings and characters, recognising that they may be from different times and places; 2Ri3 Make simple inferences from the words on the page, e.g. about feelings; 2Rw1 Comment on some vocabulary choices, e.g. adjectives; 2Rw2 Talk about what happens at the beginning, in the middle or at the end of a story.	2W03 Begin to r-read own writing aloud to check for sense and accuracy; 2W05 Use the structures of familiar poems and stories in developing own writing; 2W06 Plan writing through discussion or by speaking aloud; 2Wa4 Begin to use dialogue in stories; 2Wa7 Write simple evaluations of books read; 2Wt1 Structure a story with a beginning, middle and end; 2Wp1 Write in clear sentences using capital letters, full stops and question mark; 2Wp3 Use mainly simple and compound sentences, with 'and'/'but' to connect ideas. Because may begin to be used in a complex sentence; 2Wp4 Use past and present tenses accurately (if not always consistently); 2Ws1 Learn the different common spellings of long vowel phonemes; 2Ws2 Apply knowledge of phonemes and spelling patterns in writing independently as well as when writing sentences from memory dictated by the teacher 2Ws3 Secure the spelling of high frequency words and common irregular words; 2Ws4 Spell words with common prefixes and suffixes, e.g. *un–*, *dis–*, *–ful*, *–ly*.	2SL1 Recount experiences and explore possibilities; 2SL2 Explain plans and ideas, extending them in the light of discussion; 2SL3 Articulate clearly so that others can hear; 2SL3 Articulate clearly so that others can hear. 2SL6 Attempt to express ideas precisely, using a growing vocabulary; 2SL7 Listen carefully and respond appropriately, asking questions of others; 2SL8 Demonstrate 'attentive listening' and engage with another speaker.

Unit 5	Reading	Writing	Listening and speaking
Animals and us Texts: *Dolphin Ballet* (poem) *The Dolphin King* (traditional story from France) *Dolphins* (information text)	2R06 Read aloud with increased accuracy, fluency and expression; 2R07 Begin to read with fluency and expression, taking some notice of punctuation, including speech marks; 2R08 Explore a variety of non-fiction texts on screen; 2R10 Discuss the meaning of unfamiliar words encountered in reading; 2Rx1 Read and respond to question words, e.g. 'what', 'where', 'when', 'who', 'why'; 2Rx3 Find answers to questions by reading a section of text; 2Ri2 Identify and describe story settings and characters, recognising that they may be from different times and places; 2Ri3 Make simple inferences from the words on the page, e.g. about feelings; 2Rw1 Comment on some vocabulary choices, e.g. adjectives; 2Rw2 Talk about what happens at the beginning, in the middle or at the end of a story; 2Rv1 Show some awareness that texts have different purposes; 2Rw3 Read poems and comment on words and sounds, rhyme and rhythm.	2W03 Begin to reread own writing aloud to check for sense and accuracy;. 2W05 Use the structures of familiar poems and stories in developing own writing; 2W06 Plan writing through discussion or by speaking aloud; 2Wa4 Begin to use dialogue in stories; 2Wa7 Write simple evaluations of books read; 2Wt1 Structure a story with a beginning, middle and end; 2Wp1 Write in clear sentences using capital letters, full stops and question marks; 2Wp2 Find alternatives to 'and'/'then' in developing a narrative and connecting ideas; 2Wp3 Use mainly simple and compound sentences, with 'and'/'but' to connect ideas; 'because' may begin to be used in a complex sentence; 2Wp4 Use past and present tenses accurately (if not always consistently); 2Ws1 Learn the different common spellings of long vowel phonemes; 2Ws2 Apply knowledge of phonemes and spelling patterns in writing independently as well as when writing sentences from memory dictated by the teacher; 2Ws4 Spell words with common prefixes and suffixes, e.g. *un–*, *dis–*, *–ful*, *–ly*; 2Ws3 Secure the spelling of high frequency words and common irregular words.	2SL1 Recount experiences and explore possibilities; 2SL3 Articulate clearly so that others can hear; 2SL6 Attempt to express ideas precisely, using a growing vocabulary; 2SL7 Listen carefully and respond appropriately, asking questions of others; 2SL8 Demonstrate 'attentive listening' and engage with another speaker.

Unit 6	Reading	Writing	Listening and speaking
Staying safe Texts: *World's Deadliest Creatures* (non-fiction text)	2R06 Read aloud with increased accuracy, fluency and expression; 2R03 Identify syllables and split familiar compound words into parts; 2R04 Extend the range of common words recognised on sight; 2R05 Begin to develop likes and dislikes in reading and listening to stories drawing on background information and vocabulary provided; 2R07 Begin to read with fluency and expression, taking some notice of punctuation, including speech marks; 2R10 Discuss the meaning of unfamiliar words encountered in reading; 2Rx1 Read and respond to question words, e.g. 'what', 'where', 'when', 'who', 'why'; 2Rx3 Find answers to questions by reading a section of text; 2Rx4 Find factual information from different formats, e.g. charts, labelled diagrams; 2Rv1 Show some awareness that texts have different purposes; 2Rv2 Identify general features of known text types.	2W03 Begin to reread own writing aloud to check for sense and accuracy; 2Wa7 Write simple evaluations of books read; 2Wa3 Build and use collections of interesting and significant words; 2Wa5 Use features of chosen text type; 2Wp1 Write in clear sentences using capital letters, full stops and question marks; 2Wp3 Use mainly simple and compound sentences, with 'and'/'but' to connect ideas; 'because' may begin to be used in a complex sentence; 2Ws1 Learn the different common spellings of long vowel phonemes; 2Ws2 Apply knowledge of phonemes and spelling patterns in writing independently as well as when writing sentences from memory dictated by the teacher; 2Ws3 Secure the spelling of high frequency words and common irregular words.	2SL1 Recount experiences and explore possibilities; 2SL3 Articulate clearly so that others can hear; 2SL6 Attempt to express ideas precisely, using a growing vocabulary; 2SL7 Listen carefully and respond appropriately, asking questions of others; 2SL8 Demonstrate 'attentive listening' and engage with another speaker.

Unit 7	Reading	Writing	Listening and speaking
When Arthur Wouldn't Sleep Texts: *When Arthur Wouldn't Sleep* (real-life story about sleep and dreaming) *The Moon-Baby* (traditional African lullaby in poem form)	2R06 Read aloud with increased accuracy, fluency and expression; 2R07 Begin to read with fluency and expression, taking some notice of punctuation, including speech marks; 2R10 Discuss the meaning of unfamiliar words encountered in reading; 2Rx1 Read and respond to question words, e.g. 'what', 'where', 'when', 'who', 'why'; 2Rx3 Find answers to questions by reading a section of text; 2Ri2 Identify and describe story settings and characters, recognising that they may be from different times and places; 2Ri3 Make simple inferences from the words on the page, e.g. about feelings; 2Rw1 Comment on some vocabulary choices, e.g. adjectives; 2R03 Identify syllables and split familiar compound words into parts; 2R04 Extend the range of common words recognised on sight.	2W03 Begin to reread own writing aloud to check for sense and accuracy; 2W06 Plan writing through discussion or by speaking aloud; 2Wa1 Develop stories with a setting, characters and a sequence of events; 2Wa5 Use features of chosen text type; 2Wp1 Write in clear sentences using capital letters, full stops and question marks; 2Wp3 Use mainly simple and compound sentences, with 'and'/'but' to connect ideas; 'because may begin to be used in a complex sentence; 2Wp4 Use past and present tenses accurately (if not always consistently); 2Wp5 Begin to vary sentence openings, e.g. with simple adverbs; 2Wp6 Write with a variety of sentence types; 2Ws1 Learn the different common spellings of long vowel phonemes; 2Ws2 Apply knowledge of phonemes and spelling patterns in writing independently as well as when writing sentences from memory dictated by the teacher; 2Ws3 Secure the spelling of high frequency words and common irregular words; 2Ws4 Spell words with common prefixes and suffixes, e.g. *un–*, *dis–*, *–ful*, *–ly*	2SL1 Recount experiences and explore possibilities; 2SL3 Articulate clearly so that others can hear; 2SL6 Attempt to express ideas precisely, using a growing vocabulary; 2SL7 Listen carefully and respond appropriately, asking questions of others; 2SL8 Demonstrate 'attentive listening' and engage with another speaker; 2SL9 Extend experiences and ideas through role play.

Unit 8	Reading	Writing	Listening and speaking
The Pot of Gold Texts: *The Pot of Gold* (modern retelling of a traditional story by Julia Donaldson)	2R06 Read aloud with increased accuracy, fluency and expression; 2R07 Begin to read with fluency and expression, taking some notice of punctuation, including speech marks; 2R10 Discuss the meaning of unfamiliar words encountered in reading;. 2Rx3 Find answers to questions by reading a section of text; 2Ri2 Identify and describe story settings and characters, recognising that they may be from different times and places; 2Ri3 Make simple inferences from the words on the page, e.g. about feelings; 2Rw1 Comment on some vocabulary choices, e.g. adjectives; 2Rw2 Talk about what happens at the beginning, in the middle or at the end of a story; 2Rx1 Read and respond to question words, e.g. 'what', 'where', 'when', 'who', 'why'; 2Ri1 Predict story endings.	2W03 Begin to reread own writing aloud to check for sense and accuracy; 2W05 Use the structures of familiar poems and stories in developing own writing; 2W06 Plan writing through discussion or by speaking aloud; 2Wa2 Choose interesting words and phrases, e.g. in describing people and places; 2Wa4 Begin to use dialogue in stories; 2Wt1 Structure a story with a beginning, middle and end; 2Wp1 Write in clear sentences using capital letters, full stops and question marks; 2Wp3 Use mainly simple and compound sentences, with 'and'/'but' to connect ideas; 'because' may begin to be used in a complex sentence; 2Wp4 Use past and present tenses accurately (if not always consistently); 2Ws2 Apply knowledge of phonemes and spelling patterns in writing independently as well as when writing sentences from memory dictated by the teacher; 2Ws3 Secure the spelling of high frequency words and common irregular words.	2SL1 Recount experiences and explore possibilities; 2SL3 Articulate clearly so that others can hear; 2SL6 Attempt to express ideas precisely, using a growing vocabulary; 2SL7 Listen carefully and respond appropriately, asking questions of others; 2SL8 Demonstrate 'attentive listening' and engage with another speaker.

Unit 9	Reading	Writing	Listening and speaking
People who help us Texts: Extracts from *Fire! Fire!* (non-fiction text) Index	2R06 Read aloud with increased accuracy, fluency and expression; 2R03 Identify syllables and split familiar compound words into parts; 2R04 Extend the range of common words recognised on sight; 2R05 Begin to develop likes and dislikes in reading and listening to stories drawing on background information and vocabulary provided; 2R07 Begin to read with fluency and expression, taking some notice of punctuation, including speech marks; 2R10 Discuss the meaning of unfamiliar words encountered in reading; 2Rx1 Read and respond to question words, e.g. 'what', 'where', 'when', 'who', 'why'; 2Rx3 Find answers to questions by reading a section of text; 2Rx4 Find factual information from different formats, e.g. charts, labelled diagrams; 2Rv1 Show some awareness that texts have different purposes; 2Rv2 Identify general features of known text types.	2W03 Begin to reread own writing aloud to check for sense and accuracy; 2W06 Plan writing through discussion or by speaking aloud; 2Wa1 Develop stories with a setting, characters and a sequence of events; 2Wa3 Build and use collections of interesting and significant words; 2Wa5 Use features of chosen text type; 2Wa6 Write instructions and recount events and experiences; 2Wt4 Use a variety of simple organisational devices in non-fiction, e.g. headings, captions; 2Wp1 Write in clear sentences using capital letters, full stops and question marks; 2Wp5 Begin to vary sentence openings, e.g. with simple adverbs; 2Wp6 Write with a variety of sentence types; 2Ws2 Apply knowledge of phonemes and spelling patterns in writing independently as well as when writing sentences from memory dictated by the teacher; 2Ws3 Secure the spelling of high frequency words and common irregular words.	2SL3 Articulate clearly so that others can hear; 2SL6 Attempt to express ideas precisely, using a growing vocabulary; 2SL7 Listen carefully and respond appropriately, asking questions of others; 2SL8 Demonstrate 'attentive listening' and engage with another speaker.

Note that handwriting is not taught explicitly in this course although objectives 'W01 Form letters correctly and consistently', and 'W02 Practise handwriting patterns and the joining of letters' are implicitly covered in the activities and supporting notes in the Teacher's Guide. We recommend that teachers choose a structured and suitable course for teaching handwriting skills at Stage 2 level. *Collins Primary Focus: Handwriting* by Sue Peet, is a useful resource for this as the series progresses from introduction of fine motor movements, through pre-cursive and cursive styles at the early stages, progressing to different handwriting styles, calligraphy and links to computer fonts at the higher levels.

Unit 1 Fun and games

Unit overview

The fiction text for this unit, *Jodie the Juggler*, is a story with a familiar setting. Most learners will have some experience of things going wrong when they play with a ball or other object. The poem, *Janet the Juggler*, is a fun rhyme with alliteration and onomatopoeic language. It is an ideal poem for performing aloud. The poem *Sounds*, has strong onomatopoeic words as well as a strong rhyme.

As learners work through the unit they will have the opportunity to read, taking account of punctuation including speech marks. They will have opportunities to retell and talk about events and characters in the story.

Learners will have opportunities to learn the different common spellings of long vowels. They will look at how words can convey sounds and actions, and use interesting adjectives to write sentences.

The unit could be part of a study about actions and consequences or part of a theme on games and sports.

Reading	Writing	Listening and speaking
2R01 Learn the different ways in which vowels can be pronounced, e.g. 'how', 'low'; 'apple', 'apron';	2W03 Begin to reread own writing aloud to check for sense and accuracy;	2SL1 Recount experiences and explore possibilities;
2R02 Use phonics as the main method of tackling unfamiliar words;	2W04 Use simple non-fiction texts as a model for writing;	2SL3 Articulate clearly so that others can hear;
2R03 Identify syllables and split familiar compound words into parts;	2W05 Use the structures of familiar poems and stories in developing own writing;	2SL6 Attempt to express ideas precisely, using a growing vocabulary;
2R06 Read aloud with increased accuracy, fluency and expression;	2W07 Make simple notes from a selection of non-fiction texts, e.g. listing key words;	2SL8 Demonstrate 'attentive listening' and engage with another speaker;
2R07 Begin to read with fluency and expression, taking some notice of punctuation, including speech marks;	2Wa2 Choose interesting words and phrases, e.g. in describing people and places;	2SL9 Extend experiences and ideas through role play;
2R10 Discuss the meaning of unfamiliar words encountered in reading;	2Wa3 Build and use collections of interesting and significant words;	2SL11 Show awareness that speakers use a variety of ways of speaking in different situations and try out different ways of speaking
2Rx3 Find answers to questions by reading a section of text;	2Wa5 Use features of chosen text type;	
2Ri1 Predict story endings;	2Wt1 Structure a story with a beginning, middle and end;	
2Ri3 Make simple inferences from the words on the page, e.g. about feelings;	2Wt3 Link ideas in sections, grouped by content;	
2Rw1 Comment on some vocabulary choices, e.g. adjectives;	2Wp1 Write in clear sentences using capital letters, full stops and question marks;	
2Rw2 Talk about what happens at the beginning, in the middle or at the end of a story;	2Ws1 Learn the different common spellings of long vowel phonemes;	
2Rw3 Read poems and comment on words and sounds, rhyme and rhythm.	2Ws2 Apply knowledge of phonemes and spelling patterns in writing independently as well as when writing sentences from memory dictated by the teacher from memory.	

Related resources:

- Slideshow 1: Fun and games
- Audio files: *Jodie the Juggler*; *Janet the Juggler*
- PCM 1: Phonics *a–e*
- PCM 2: Phonics *ai, ay, a–e*
- PCM 3: Phonics *o–e*
- PCM 4: Compound words
- PCM 5: Contractions
- PCM 6: End of unit assessment

Introducing the unit

Ask learners to tell each other what games, sport and fun activities they took part in during the school holidays. Choose three or four learners and ask them to tell the rest of the class about their favourite holiday activity.

Display pictures of potentially dangerous adventure sports (rock climbing, big wave surfing, motor racing, skateboarding and mountain trail biking). Discuss each sport and talk about what the participants do to stay safe (protective gear, safety precautions, choosing safe places to do the sport and so on).

Point out that things can go wrong in adventure sports, for example: racing cars may crash, or skateboarders may fall and hurt themselves. Allow learners to tell you about any 'sport disasters' they know of. Next, introduce the idea that things can go wrong in almost any type of sport or game, for example: a cricket ball could break a window. Spend some time talking about learners' own experiences of things going wrong when they are playing at home or school. Discuss what they did when these things happened.

Week 1

Student's Book pages 1–6

Workbook pages 1–2

Student's Book pages 1–4

Tell learners that they are going to read a story about a little boy called Jodie who can juggle. Ask learners if they know what juggling means and if any of them can juggle.

Read the text on page 1 together. Model how to use the picture (a flying orange) and the grammar of the broken sentence ('He juggled with three oranges and … he broke a cup.') to help predict the next event.

Go through the rest of the story, looking at the pictures and discussing what is happening. How does Jodie's mum try to stop Jodie juggling? Point out the use of speech bubbles as part of the story.

Ask learners to read the story quietly and independently. Monitor by asking individual learners to read aloud. Check that learners are using a range of strategies to tackle unknown words: looking at the pictures, sounding out words, using context and grammatical clues, reading on and rereading.

Support: During this time, work with a group of learners who need more direct support to apply strategies.

Draw the class together and invite individuals to read while others follow the text.

Highlight and praise strategies used to decipher any new or unfamiliar words.

Spend as much time as necessary with individuals or groups to ensure accurate decoding.

After reading, ask questions to check understanding. For example:

- What did Jodie like doing?
- Did Jodie's mother like Jodie to juggle?
- What did Jodie's mother want him to do?
- Whose house did Jodie go to?
- What was Jodie's mother doing when he went back to his own flat?

Discuss with learners how Jodie's mother felt and how Asif's father felt.

Discuss if the story had a happy ending. Was everybody happy in the end? Had Jodie's mother's plan worked?

Student's Book page 5

Reading and understanding

1 Learners are asked to find and write the answers to 'who', 'what' and 'where' questions. Highlight these words and discuss with learners what type of answer is needed for each. For example, a 'who' question will need the name of a person(s) for the answer; a 'where' question will need the name of a place in the answer, for example: 'at the beach', 'in the house'.

Remind learners about capital letters and full stops in sentences. Also remind them to refer back to the text to check accuracy of answers and spelling.

Extension: Learners could write some questions using the question words 'who', 'where' and 'what'. Remind them to use a capital letter at the beginning and a question mark at the end.

2 Before learners turn to the task, discuss how you can tell if someone is happy, for example: body language, facial expression, how they speak and what they say.

Ask learners to think of a mood, for example: happy, sad, tired, excited, grumpy, frightened, and so on. Invite learners in turn to show their chosen mood to their peers through facial expression and body language. Their peers could then suggest words that would suit the chosen mood.

Answers
1 juggling; play football outside; Asif; the park; Dom, Sue and Ash.
2 They smiled at Jodie.
They said nice things about him.
They stood beside him.

Listening and speaking

Observe learners as they work in pairs to discuss how Jodie's mother felt at different times in the story. Make sure they are taking turns and listening to each other.

Student's Book page 6

Reading and writing

1 Before turning to the activity, ask the learners to find what certain characters said. For example:

- What did Asif's dad say? (page 7)
- What did Jodie's mum say? (page 13)
- What did Dom, Sue and Ash say? (page 13)
- What did Jodie say? (page 15)

Write one or two of the sentences on the whiteboard using different coloured pens for the exact words that the character said, for example: "Can we borrow your football?" they asked.

2–3 Before turning to these activities, ask learners to work in pairs and create a dialogue that the man and Jodie might have had after the glass was broken. Invite pairs of learners to role-play their dialogue to their peers.

Answers
Mum; Asif's dad; Mum; Jodie; Dom; Ash; Sue; Mum; Jodie

Workbook pages 1–2

Writing

In this activity, learners find in the story something that each character said. They then write what the character said in the speech bubble.

Focus on the example that has been done and elicit how the words are written without speech marks when they are written in a speech bubble.

Possible answers
1 Jodie:
Yes. I don't like football. But I'll try one kick first.
I don't want to juggle any more. I want to play football.
Sorry, Mum. Lucky that man gave us our ball back.
Dom:
Can we borrow your football?
BRILLIANT kick!
Jodie's mum:
Jodie, go outside and play football.
JODIE, STOP JUGGLING!
No juggling!
Jodie, we're going to the park to play football NOW!
Jodie, we're going home.
Maybe juggling is a good idea. I'll make you some juggling bags.
Sue:
Can we borrow your football?
You're a STAR!
2 Learners' own answers.

Weekly review

Use this rubric to assess learners' progress as they worked through the activities this week.

Level	Reading
■	This group are beginning to read aloud with increased accuracy. They read and can respond to question words.
●	This group are beginning to read aloud with increased accuracy, fluency and expression. They read and can respond to question words.
▲	This group read aloud with increased accuracy, fluency and expression. They read and respond well to question words.

Week 2

Student's Book pages 7–8

Workbook pages 2–4

Workbook pages 2–3

Sounds and spelling

This activity should come after focused teaching sessions about the different representations of the long vowel sound *a*.

Ask learners to turn to pages 1–4 in the Student's Book, and find the word 'play' on each of the story frames 2, 7, 9 and 15 in turn.

Ask learners what sound they hear at the end of the word 'play' and how it is represented. Confirm the long vowel sound *a* and that it is written *ay*.

Ask learners how many sounds they can hear in the word 'play' and confirm there are three – *p-l-ay*. Write the word 'play' on the whiteboard.

Then ask learners, in turn, to write down other words that rhyme with 'play'. Then collect their words on the whiteboard underneath the word 'play'.

Suggested words: 'clay', 'tray', 'stay', 'fray', 'sway', 'pray', 'bay', 'day', 'gay', 'lay', 'hay', 'may', 'pay', 'ray', 'say', 'way'.

Ask learners to read the lists of words and to say what they notice about them. Confirm that they all have *ay* at the end and they all rhyme.

Answers
1 tray; cake; train; snail; chain; plate
2 Learners' own answers.

Dictation

Use these or similar sentences for dictation to reinforce and assess spelling in this unit.

• Sanjay and Kay went out to play.
• Gran will pay on the bus.
• The milk jug is on the tray.
• We ran a long way.
• It was a wet day.

Once this work has been done, make some time, either now or later, to ask learners what the other representation of the long vowel sound is (*ai*). Invite learners to give examples of words with *ai* in them, for example: 'stain', 'train', 'gain', 'drain', 'faint', 'paint'.

Ask learners where they usually hear the long vowel sound *a* represented by *ai* in words and confirm the middle.

Ask learners where they usually hear the long vowel sound *a* represented by *ay* in words and confirm the end.

Give learners opportunities to identify where they hear the long vowel sound *a* in words, and how it is written when it is in the middle and when it is at the end of words.

Each learner will need: a piece of card/paper with *ai* written on it; a piece of card with *ay* written on it; or a mini-whiteboard and marker.

1 Learners point to/hold up the correct card or piece of paper with the letters representing the long vowel sound *a* (*ai* or *ay*) written on it when the teacher says a word.

2 Learners should write *ai* or *ay* when the teacher says a word.

Suggested words: 'day', 'gain', 'tray', 'clay', 'train', 'may', 'stain', 'rain', 'wait', 'hay', 'spray', 'nail', 'pail', 'play', 'sail', 'drain', 'stay', 'way', 'paint', 'tail', 'pay'.

Give learners opportunities to practise the 'join' of *ay* and *ai*. This reinforces the fact that the two letters make one sound.

Learners should use colour to indicate the 'joins' when writing the words.

The above words should be dictated for the learners to write.

Ask learners to turn to page 6 of the story, to read the text and identify any word that has the long vowel sound a written in a different way. Confirm 'plate'.

Then ask them to read page 8 of the story and to identify any words with the long vowel sound *a*. Confirm 'cake' and 'late'. Repeat for page 14 and the word 'make'.

Write the words 'plate', 'cake', 'late' and 'make' on the whiteboard and ask learners what they notice about the words. For example:

- two pairs of rhyming words – 'plate' and 'late', 'cake' and 'bake'
- a different way of writing the long vowel sound *a*.

Tell the learners that when e comes at the end of a word, as in 'plate', the vowel in the middle says its name and not its sound, and the e at the end is silent. For example: 'tap' – 'tap*e*'; 'man' – 'man*e*'; 'can' – 'can*e*'; 'mad' – 'mad*e*'; 'hat' – 'hat*e*'; 'mat' – 'mat*e*'.

Tell learners that you want to write the word 'came' and ask them how many sounds they can hear in the word 'came'. Confirm three, *c-a-m* with a silent e at the end – 'came' – and write 'came' on the board. Remind learners that the e must go at the end to make the vowel long (it says its name and not its sound).

Repeat for other rhyming words: 'fame', 'game', 'lame', 'name', 'same', 'tame'.

Other words to investigate, read and spell are: 'bake', 'cake', 'lake', 'make', 'take', 'wake', 'shake', 'flake', 'snake'; 'date', 'gate', 'hate', 'late', 'mate', 'plate', 'skate'; 'cave', 'gave', 'save', 'wave', 'grave'.

You should point out that *a–e* is more often used to make the long vowel sound *a* where the consonant is *m* (*–ame*), *k* (*–ake*), *v* (*–ave*), or *t* (*–ate*). While *ai* represents the same sound, it is not as common with these consonants. Exceptions are 'wait', 'bait' and 'gait'.

Use PCMs 1 and 2 to test learners' work on these spellings.

Support: Some learners may find it easier to use magnetic letters for spelling words. This allows them to focus on spelling without having to think how to form the letters. This is particularly beneficial to learners with fine motor skill difficulties needed for handwriting.

Extension: Able learners could investigate other representations of the long vowel sound *a*, such as *ea*, as in 'great' and 'break'; *ei* as in 'neighbour' and 'weigh'.

Dictation
These sentences use the *a–e* spelling.

- Dad left a cake on the plate.
- Mum came to the park with me.
- I gave Jade a book.
- The dog hid in the cave.
- The snake is on the rock

These sentences use *ay*, *a–e* or *ai*.

- We went a long way on the train.
- Meg will wait at the gate.
- Ben has a cake on a tray.
- They went out to play in the rain.
- The snail is on the rake.
- Dad will take the paint to the shed.

Workbook pages 3–4

Sounds and spelling
The focus of this activity is the different representations of the long vowel sound *o*.

Ask learners to think of the different ways that the long vowel *o* is usually written (*oa* as in 'b*oa*t', usually found in the middle of words; *ow* as in 'gl*ow*', usually found at the end of words).

Now, give learners opportunities to identify where they hear the long vowel sound *o* in words, and how it is written when it is in the middle and when it is at the end of words.

Each learner will need: a piece of card/paper with *oa* written on it; a piece of card with *ow* written on it; or a mini-whiteboard and marker.

1 They point to/hold up the correct card or piece of paper with the letters representing the long vowel sound *o* (*oa* or *ow*) written on it when the teacher says a word.

2 They write *oa* or *ow* when the teacher says a word.

Suggested words: 'load', 'mow', 'throat', 'foam', 'crow', 'toad', 'throw', 'snow', 'foal', 'coast', 'show', 'coach', 'low', 'loan', 'roast', 'blow', 'tow', 'coat', 'grow', 'boast', 'groan', 'flow', 'road', 'bow'.

Ask learners to turn to page 2 of the Student's Book, to read the text and identify any word that has the long vowel sound o written in a different way. Confirm 'broke'. This word has a different way of writing the long vowel sound o.

Tell learners that when e comes at the end of a word, as in 'broke', the vowel in the middle says its name and not its sound, and the e at the end is silent. For example: 'hop' – 'hope'; 'rob' – 'robe'; 'rod' – 'rode'; 'not' – 'note'.

Tell learners that you want to write the word 'pole' and ask them how many sounds they can hear in the word 'pole'. Confirm three, p-o-l with a silent e at the end – 'pole' – and write 'pole' on the board. Remind learners that the e must go at the end to make the vowel long (it says its name and not its sound).

Repeat for other rhyming words: 'mole', 'hole', 'sole', 'stole'.

Other words to investigate, read and spell: 'coke', 'joke', 'poke', 'woke', 'broke', 'spoke', 'smoke', 'choke', 'hose', 'nose', 'rose', 'close', 'bone', 'cone', 'stone', 'hope', 'rope', 'slope', 'code'.

While oa and o–e represent the same sound, point out that o–e is more often used to make the long vowel sound o where the consonant is k (–oke), s (–ose), or p (–ope). Exceptions are 'soap', 'oak', 'soak', 'cloak'.

PCM 3 gives additional practice using the long o sound.

Extension: Able learners could investigate other representations of the long vowel sound o, such as: o in 'go' and 'so'; oe as in 'toe', 'hoe', 'doe', 'foe', 'Joe'. Remind learners that changing the onset in 'toe' will help make other words that rhyme with 'toe'.

Dictation
These sentences test the o–e sound.
- The rope is long.
- Fred broke his arm.
- I fell on a stone and cut my hand.
- The rose has a strong smell.
- The smoke is thick and black.

These sentences test the oa, ow and o–e sounds.
- My coat has a hole in it.
- A stone is on the road.
- I hope the raft will float.
- Joan will row the boat.

- I have a bone stuck in my throat.

Answers
1 coat; bone; road; bow; rope; window.
2 Learners' own answers.

Student's Book page 7
Sounds and spelling
Before turning to activity 1, refer to page 7 of the Student's Book and ask learners to follow as you read what Asif's dad said: "Boys, go outside and play football."

Clap on the words as you say them, with two claps for the compound words.

Invite learners to identify the two words in each compound word: 'out/side', 'foot/ball'.

Emphasise the term 'compound word' and establish that a compound word consists of two smaller words joined together to make one word.

Display some word cards. Each card should have a word on it that can be joined with another to make a compound word.

Examples include: 'play', 'ground', 'time', 'farm', 'house', 'yard', 'arm', 'wheel', 'chair', 'sea', 'side', 'foot', 'net', 'ball', 'up', 'down', 'stairs', 'day', 'time', 'break', 'night', 'out', 'side'.

Ask learners to find two words that together make a compound word. Leaners clap on each part of the compound word as they say it.

Give learners some practice in spelling compound words. Ask them to split the compound word into its component parts and spell each part using spelling rules they already know. Use PCM 4 for this purpose.

In activity 2, learners are asked to use high frequency words to complete sentences.

This should be a part of ongoing practice of learning to spell high frequency words. Remind learners to look at any tricky parts of words and to ask themselves what strategy might help.

Some strategies that can help:
- using knowledge of phonemes and segmenting words into phonemes for spelling
- using knowledge of onset and rime – knowing the spelling of one word can help with another
- letter patterns and strings – practise common letter patterns and strings such as –ing, –ight

- break words into syllables
- use mnemonics, for example, 'difficulty': Mr D, Mr I, Mr FFI, Mr C, Mr U, Mr LTY
- use the 'look, say, write, cover and check' method. Learners need to get into the habit of looking at words with intent: observing details, highlighting difficult parts, visualising and committing the word to memory.

Extension: Investigate contractions like 'don't' with able learners by building upon learners' use of contractions in speech and promoting how to use them in spelling. Emphasise that the apostrophe replaces missing letters and must be placed precisely. PCM 5 covers this topic.

Suggested words: 'cannot' – 'can't'; 'he is' – 'he's'; 'do not' – 'don't'; 'she is' – 'she's'; 'I am' – 'I'm'; 'is not' – 'isn't'; 'does not' – 'doesn't'.

Answers
1 teaspoon, supermarket, upstairs, seesaw, grandmother, butterfly, handwriting, firework, forget
2 He kicked the ball as hard as he could.
It smashed some glass.
I don't like football.

Student's Book page 8

Reading and writing
1–2 Learners are asked to write lists: firstly, things that Jodie juggled with, and secondly, things that Jodie broke. Ask them to read the text again before making the two lists, and to refer back to the text to check answers and spellings after they have written the lists.

3 Learners are asked to write sentences in the correct order – the order that Jodie did them in. Remind learners that when they have finished, they should read what they have written and check if it is in the correct order.

Listening and speaking
Learners should work in pairs and talk about what happened next. (Jodie left Asif's flat and went back to his own flat.) Encourage learners to include as much detail as possible in their dialogue.

Invite a member from each pair of learners to tell what happened.

Writing
Learners then write the next part of the story, that is when Jodie went back to his own flat.

Answers
1 socks, shoes, three oranges, three flowerpots, three apples, three eggs
2 a cup, flowerpots, a plate, three eggs, some glass
3 He juggled with oranges. He broke the flowerpots. He went to Asif's flat. He juggled with apples. He broke a plate.

Weekly review
Use this rubric to assess learners' progress as they worked through the activities this week.

Level	Reading	Writing
■	This group use phonics as the main method of tackling unfamiliar words and with some support are becoming more confident at recognising the different representations of the long vowels *a* and *o*.	This group can spell words with the different representations of the long vowels *a* and *o* when the words are in lists with the same spelling pattern.
●	This group use phonics as the main method of tackling unfamiliar words and recognise the different representations of the long vowels *a* and *o* most of the time.	This group can spell words with the different representations of the long vowels *a* and *o* and apply their knowledge of phonemes and spelling patterns in writing most of the time.
▲	This group use phonics as the main method of tackling unfamiliar words and recognise the different representations of the long vowels *a* and *o*.	This group can spell words with the different representations of the long vowels *a* and *o* and apply their knowledge of phonemes and spelling patterns in writing.

Week 3

Student's Book pages 9–11

Workbook pages 4–8

Workbook page 4

Reading and writing

This section takes learners to the last part of the story, i.e. when his mum took Jodie to the park. Learners imagine that they are Jodie, telling Asif what happened at the park. Encourage learners to read their story when they have finished and check if it makes sense. An alternative could be to read and check a partner's work.

Answers

park, football, and, came, football, kicked, glass, pleased, home, I don't want to juggle anymore. I want to play football

Workbook page 5

Sounds and spelling

These activities focus on the letter string *ar*. The sound represented by *ar* sounds like the name of the alphabet letter *R*.

Tell learners that when *r* comes after the vowel *a* (to make *ar*) and is in the middle or the end of a word, the sound *ar* sounds like the alphabet letter *R* (name).

Note: A 'letter string' is a sequence of letters that occurs frequently. Learners will already be familiar with some letter strings and where they are most likely to appear in words, for example: *ay, oa, ight*.

Discuss with learners letters that often appear together in words, for example: *sh, ch, th, oo, ee, igh, ar*.

Answers

1 park, car, stars, card, jar, shark
2 Learners' own answers.
3 tart, March, market

Student's Book page 9

Reading and speaking

Let the learners work in pairs to discuss the title and then read the poem. Encourage them to read it with expression and actions.

Give learners time to share what they liked or did not like about the poem before asking for some contributions as a class.

Workbook page 6

Speaking and listening

Before turning to the activity, invite learners to look at and comment on how the word 'CRASH!' is written on pages 2, 3, 6 and 12 of the story. Discuss with learners why it is written like that.

Ask learners to say another word in the story ('SPLAT!', page 8) that is written in the same way (i.e. to suggest a sound).

1 Give learners time to work with a partner and talk about the onomatopoeic words. What do the words suggest to the learners? Then draw learners together to say what they think the words suggest.

2 Learners are asked to match sentences to words that describe the action.

Answers

1 Learners' own answers.

2

a plate being dropped on the floor	smash
a balloon being burst	pop
a light being switched on	click
water going down a drain	gurgle
coins making a noise in your pocket	jingle
a rocket taking off	whoosh
a flag blowing in the breeze	flutter

Student's Book page 10

Reading and writing

1 Learners are asked to use onomatopoeic words to complete sentences.

2 Learners are asked to choose an onomatopoeic word, draw a picture that illustrates each of the given onomatopoeic words, and then to write a caption for each. Before turning to the activity, discuss with learners what the words suggest to them and choose one word to model what is being asked.

Support: Work with individuals or a small group of learners and discuss their pictures and what captions they might write. Scribe any captions if necessary.

1 The door creaked when it opened.; The rocket zoomed into space.; The pots and pans clattered onto the floor.; The fire crackled as it burned.; The girl honked the horn on the bike.
2 Learners' own answers.

Workbook page 7

Reading and writing

This short poem gives learners the opportunity to experience poetry with onomatopoeic language.

1 Read the poem with the learners, highlighting the sounds, the rhyme and the rhythm.

2 Learners are asked to write words that suggest sounds.

3 Learners are asked to write pairs of rhyming words.

4 Learners are asked to use the structure of a familiar poem to complete a new verse for the poem.

Before learners turn to this activity, spend time with them discussing vocabulary that would fit in with the style of the poem. You might choose to write a 'class' verse for the poem.

Answers
2 whistling, pattering, tapping, splashing, gurgling,
3 rain – drain, pane – lane
4 Learners' own answers.

Student's Book page 11

Reading and writing

Before turning to the activity ask learners to choose a word to describe their socks (or another item of clothing). Some further

examples could be used, for example: adjectives to describe hair, weather, food.

Establish with the learners that words that describe things (nouns) are called 'adjectives'.

Using objects within the classroom, for example, a pencil, a bag, a cupboard, ask learners to choose an adjective to describe each. For example: a short/long/red pencil; a small/big/bag; a tall/small/old cupboard.

1 Learners are asked to write a list of words that describe socks. They can use the pictures to help them think of some words of their own.

2 Learners are asked to write a sentence describing their favourite socks from the pictures.

3 Learners are asked to add adjectives to complete sentences and then to copy the sentences.

Answers
1 striped, spotted, pink, blue, red, patterned, new, odd, torn
2 Learners' own answers.
3 Learners' own answers.

Extension: Ask learners to write a description of an item (choose things they are interested in). They can exchange descriptions and use them to draw the item their partner has described.

Workbook page 8

Reading and writing

In this activity, learners are asked to complete the table to show which game broke the most things. An example is given in the juggling column. Remind learners that they should draw the objects and write the name for each, for example: 'three eggs'.

Weekly review

Use this rubric to assess learners' progress as they worked through the activities this week.

Level	Reading	Listening and speaking
■	This group comment well on words that suggest sounds and enjoyed reading them with expression.	This group listen well most of the time but at times need teacher support to respond appropriately.
●	This group comment well on vocabulary choices and are beginning to show understanding of why the author chose certain words.	This group listen carefully for most of the time, and respond appropriately.
▲	This group comment well on vocabulary choices. They show understanding of why the author chose certain words.	This group listen carefully at all times, and respond appropriately.

End of unit assessment

Use PCM 6 to review and informally assess how well learners have understood the concept of descriptive onomatopoeic words and to see if they are able to use strongly descriptive words correctly in sentences. Let learners exchange completed sheets and check each other's work.

Unit 2 The Olympics

Unit overview

As the learners work through the unit they will work with a range of non-fiction texts presented in different ways.

This unit provides a set of non-fiction texts giving a short history of the Olympics, and then a focus on the 2012 Summer Olympics in London. Some of the information is presented in the form of charts and tables. A short biographical text is also presented (Usain Bolt). A simple glossary activity is included to develop skills in locating information. In addition to the text in the Student's Book, the learners will explore on-screen information about the Olympics.

The unit could be part of a study of sport and a healthy lifestyle.

Learners will have the opportunity to revisit and secure the different representations for the long vowel *e* and *u*. They will also learn about *oi* and *oy* representing the same sound in words.

Reading	Writing	Listening and speaking
2R02 Use phonics as the main method of tackling unfamiliar words;	2W04 Use simple non-fiction texts as a model for writing;	2SL1 Recount experiences and explore possibilities;
2R04 Extend the range of common words recognised on sight;	2W07 Make simple notes from a selection of non-fiction texts, e.g. listing key words;	2SL8 Demonstrate 'attentive listening' and engage with another speaker;
2R06 Read aloud with increased accuracy, fluency and expression;	2Wa2 Choose interesting words and phrases, e.g. in describing people and places;	2SL6 Attempt to express ideas precisely, using a growing vocabulary
2R07 Begin to read with fluency and expression, taking some notice of punctuation, including speech marks;	2Wa3 Build and use collections of interesting and significant words;	
2R08 Explore a variety of non-fiction texts on screen;	2Wa5 Use features of chosen text type;	
2R09 Locate words by initial letter in simple dictionaries, glossaries and indexes;	2Wt1 Structure a story with a beginning, middle and end;	
2R10 Discuss the meaning of unfamiliar words encountered in reading;	2Wt4 Use a variety of simple organisational devices in non-fiction, e.g. headings, captions;	
2Rx2 Read and follow simple instructions, e.g. in a recipe;	2Wp1 Write in clear sentences using capital letters, full stops and question marks;	
2Rx3 Find answers to questions by reading a section of text;	2Ws1 Learn the different common spellings of long vowel phonemes;	
2Rx4 Find factual information from different formats, e.g. charts, labelled diagrams;	2Ws2 Apply knowledge of phonemes and spelling patterns in writing independently as well as when writing sentences from memory dictated by the teacher;	
2Rv1 Show some awareness that texts have different purposes;		
2Rv2 Identify general features of known text types	2Ws3 Secure the spelling of high frequency words and common irregular words	

Related resources:

- Slideshow 2: The Olympics
- Audio files: *The Olympic Games*; *Usain Bolt*
- PCM 7: Glossary words
- PCM 8: Phonics *ew*
- PCM 9: Phonics *u–e*
- PCM 10: Write instructions
- PCM 11: End of unit assessment

Introducing the unit

Show the class flags from different countries, plus your own country's flag. Ask them try to name the countries represented. If they are not sure, allow them to try and find the flags in the unit and identify them that way.

Spend some time discussing where we see flags on display and what they represent.

Explain that when a group of people represent their country in some way, they usually do so under the country's flag. The Olympic Games is one event where athletes take part under a country flag. Usually their sporting gear for the event is also in the colours of the flag.

Tell the class they are going to learn more about the Olympic Games in this unit. Spend some time discussing what they already know before moving on. Bear in mind that the 2016 Olympic Games will take place in Rio de Janeiro in Brazil and as this event gets closer, there will be lots of information available to supplement your classroom resources

---

Week 1

Student's Book pages 12–14

Workbook pages 9–10

Student's Book pages 12–13

Reading

Ask learners what kind of books they would use to find information about the Olympic Games. Then talk about how non-fiction books are structured to make it easy to locate information. Show the class some examples and recap features such as contents page, index, glossary, headings, diagrams, tables and any other features the learners know. Discuss briefly where else you could find information about the games including the internet, newspapers and TV programmes.

Before asking learners to skim read the text, remind them that skim reading is a surface look to find out more about what the text contains. It is not a detailed reading of the information. Elicit from learners how photographs, drawings, diagrams and charts can give information when you skim read.

Place learners in groups and give them time to read the text together. Discuss any 'tricky' words and establish meaning, for example, 'legend'. Model correct reading.

Support: Support individuals or small groups by drawing their attention to the headings and the illustrations and showing how these can help with the reading of the text.

After the learners have read the information, draw them together to highlight and discuss the main points from each page by asking the learners to show where in the text they will find out about:

- the modern Olympic Games
- the colours that make up the Olympic flag
- sports that are in the Olympics
- the first Olympic Games
- the Olympic medals.

Ask learners how they knew which section of the text to look at to find out about the different things (the 'headings'). Ask some questions about information in each section, checking that the learners are looking in the correct section for the answer. For example:

- Where were the first Olympics held?
- What are the six colours that are in the Olympic flag?
- Where do the winners stand to get their medals?
- What is special about the years that the summer Olympics are held?
- What sport would be held at the winter Olympics?
- Why do you think some sports can only be held in the winter?

If necessary, reread the text with the learners, again spending as much time as necessary to ensure correct decoding and understanding of text.

Workbook page 9

Reading

This activity highlights some of the key vocabulary associated with the Olympics and used in the text. Learners will be familiar with the vocabulary through earlier reading and discussing of the text. However, check that they can read the words, which are now out of context, before they complete the task of matching the words to the pictures.

Student's Book page 14

Reading and writing

1 Learners are asked to reread the text and answer questions. Encourage the learners to refer back to the text to check accuracy of answers and spellings.

2–3 Learners should then complete Activities 2 and 3. If they are interested, allow them to carry out research to find different country flags from the ones they already know.

Speaking and writing

If possible, access the 2016 Olympic Games website and look at the advertisement for 2016 games. Read a little about the 2016 Games with the class. If not, encourage learners to do their own research online.

1 Give learners some time to talk about what an ancient poster might have looked like, what the poster might have been made of and so on.

2 Learners should make a list of what might have been written on the poster.

3 Learners design their own advertisement for the first Olympic Games.

Answers

1 Olympia in Greece; an olive wreath; 1896; America, Europe, Asia, Africa and Australia; red, yellow, green, blue, black and white

Workbook page 10

Sounds and spelling

Using the word 'hoist' as a link, the activity focuses on the alternative spellings for the vowel phoneme represented by *oi* and *oy*.

Use written examples such as: They will hoist the flag of the gold medallist; The boy watched the medal ceremony.

Ask learners to identify words that have the same sound written in two different ways, i.e. 'hoist' and' boy'.

Practise auditory discrimination by inviting the learners to identify where they hear the sound in words. Is it in the middle or at the end of the word?

Examples: 'coin', 'boy', 'join', 'coil', 'toy', 'Roy', 'hoist', 'boil'.

Note: *Oi* is used in the middle of words and *oy* at the end of words or at the end of a syllable in multi-syllable words. See the Extension work for more able learners.

Give learners practice in identifying where they hear the sound – in the middle or at the end of words and what the representation of the sound is.

Each learner will need: a piece of card/paper with *oi* written on it, a piece of card with *oy* written on it, or a mini-whiteboard and marker.

1 Learners point to/hold up the correct card or piece of paper with the letters *oy* or *oi* written on it when the teacher says a word.

2 Learners write *oi* or *oy* when the teacher says a word.

Suggested words: 'hoist', 'Troy', 'join', 'coy', 'boy', 'point', 'joint', 'toy', 'annoy', 'coin', 'enjoy', 'destroy', 'spoil', 'moist'.

Give the learners practice in writing the 'joins' of *oy* and *oi*. Learners should use colour to indicate the 'joins' when writing words.

Dictation

Use these or similar sentences for dictation to reinforce the *oy* and *oi* spellings.

- The coin is in the bank.
- The coil was made of steel.
- The soil in the tub is wet.
- The boy came to play with me.
- The car needs oil.
- Roy and his dog went to the park.

Extension: Ask able learners to investigate words like 'royal', 'loyal', 'oyster', 'voyage'. Although *oy* does not appear at the end of the words it is at the end of the first syllable. Discuss with learners the spelling of the first syllable of each word i.e. *oy*.

Answers

1 hoist and moist; joint and point; join and coin; foil and coil/boil
2 toy, boy, joy
3 middle: soil, coin, join; end: toy, boy, Roy

Weekly review

Use this rubric to assess learners' progress as they worked through the activities this week.

Level	Reading
■	This group can read and find factual information from different formats with support.
●	With minimal support this group can read and find factual information from different formats.
▲	This group can read and find factual information from different formats.

Week 2

Student's Book pages 15–16

Workbook pages 11–14

Before the learners turn to the activities on Workbook page 11 and Student's Book page 15, ask them what sports they know that are in the Olympics. Make a list on the whiteboard. Discuss different sports and what is involved in each sport. Are they individual or team sports? Winter or summer sports? Discuss why there might be more summer Olympic sports than winter Olympic sports.

Workbook page 11

Reading

In this activity learners match pictures of sports to their names.

Student's Book page 15

Writing

Before learners turn to this activity, discuss the images. Ask what is happening, how the competitors might be feeling/thinking, and discuss the vocabulary pertinent to each picture.

Invite learners in turn to say what is happening in the pictures, invite other learners to comment sensitively and suggest how good sentences could be made even better. Model sentences if necessary.

Before the learners turn to the activity, remind them that they should write in sentences, using capital letters and full stops.

Support: Support individuals or small groups of learners by asking them to say what is happening in each picture and what sentence they could write. Help them to write their sentences as necessary.

Workbook pages 12–13

Sounds and spelling

Using the word 'team' invite learners to say what sound they hear in the middle of the word 'team'. They will already know that the long vowel sound e can be represented by ee. Tell the learners that the long vowel sound e can also be represented by ea.

Suggested words: 'each', 'beach', 'peach', 'reach', 'teach', 'eat', 'beat', 'heat', 'meat', 'neat', 'seat', 'team', 'cream', 'dream', 'steam', 'lean', 'mean', 'clean', 'bead', 'lead', 'read'.

Tell learners that they need to learn to use the correct spelling ee or ea and how important it is for words like 'see'/'sea'.

Write the words 'see' and 'sea' on the whiteboard and, through discussion, elicit why it is important to use the correct spelling in the sentences:

* I can see the bus.
* I can swim in the sea.

The wrong choice of spelling will change the meaning of the sentences.

Note: 'See' and 'sea' are homophones. Homophones are words which sound the same but have different spellings.

There are a number of other homophones which the learners should learn to spell and know the meanings of at this stage. For example: week/weak; meet/meat; reed/read; been/bean; seem/seam; peel/peal; reel/real; tee/tea; beech/beach; deer/dear; steel/steal.

The long vowel is usually represented by ee or ea. The learners need a lot of exposure to seeing these words in context as it can be difficult to know which representation to use. There are no guidelines as to which to use. Almost all words with the long e sound are spelt ee or ea. Words should be learnt and the learners given the opportunity to practise

33

✓

writing the words, which should always be given in the context of a sentence.

Dictation

got meat from the shop.

We have been in the sea.

Glen had beans to eat.

The sick man feels weak.

I am six next week.

We will meet on the train.

I have a book to read in my room.

1 Learners are asked to write *ea* words.

2 The learners are asked to write *ee* words with rhyming patterns.

3 Learners are asked to choose the correct word to complete sentences.

Answers
1 seal, peach, beads
2 Learners' own answers.
3 week, read, sea

Extension:

1 Learners could investigate other representations of the sound, i.e. *ey* as in 'key', *e–e* as in 'eve', and high frequency words like 'me', 'be', 'we', 'he' and 'she'.

2 Learners could further investigate homophones, for example: 'right'/'write', 'pear'/'pair', 'hear'/'here', 'there'/'their'.

Take the opportunity to practise auditory discrimination by checking if learners can accurately identify short vowels and long vowels in words.

Say words and invite the learners to answer 'short vowel' or 'long vowel'.

Examples: 'pen', 'teeth', 'vest', 'read', 'team', 'leg', 'peel', 'get', 'ten', 'sleep', 'peach', 'tree', 'men'.

Student's Book page 16

Reading and writing

1 This activity asks learners to answer 'When', 'What' and 'How many' questions. Recap these question words and what kind of answers they need and how the answers should be written, for example, by using number symbols for answers related to dates.

2–3 Give learners some time to work with a partner and read the information given in a

poster, and to check their understanding of the meanings of the words 'venue' and 'competitors'. Encourage learners to use other words in the text to help with meaning. For example: can '1160 men, 1071 women' help them to work out what the meaning of 'competitors' might be?

Before turning to activity 4, discuss with the learners what might be on the poster, the layout and the style, referring to information on the athletics poster if appropriate.

4 Using the poster in activity 2 as a guide, the learners plan and write a poster for a sports event at their school.

Answers
1 2012; 27 July; 12 August; three times, 1908, 1948, 2012; 80,000.

Tell learners that non-fiction books often have a glossary placed at the end of the book. A glossary is a list of unusual or difficult words in alphabetical order, and their meanings. Refer to glossaries in books from your class library.

Revise alphabetical order by asking questions such as:

- Which word would come first: 'book' or 'paper'; 'tiger' or 'elephant'?
- Which word would come first: 'cup', 'spoon' or 'plate'; 'gate', 'door' or 'house'; 'train', 'boat' or 'lorry'?

Next, hand out PCM 7 and explain to learners that they need to make up a glossary for a book about the Olympic Games. The words and the meanings are given but they do not match. Learners should cut out the words and their meanings, place the words in alphabetical order and match the correct meaning to each word.

Before learners turn to the task, read the words and their meanings with them to ensure correct decoding.

Workbook pages 13–14

Sounds and spelling

Tell learners that they need to listen for the sound at the end of the words that you are going to say: 'few', 'new', 'crew', 'stew', 'chew'.

Ask what sound they hear, and confirm the long vowel sound *u*.

Ask learners how this sound is usually written if it is in the middle of a word (*oo* as in 'room'). Tell learners that if the long vowel sound *u* is at the end of a word it is usually represented by *ew*.

Exceptions: 'blue', 'clue', 'due', 'glue', 'true'.

Note: *Ue* is usually used at the end of words of more than one syllable like 'avenue', 'statue', 'revenue'.

Tell learners that you want to write the word 'few' and ask them how many sounds they can hear. Confirm two – *f-ew* – and write the word 'few' on the whiteboard. Repeat the procedure for 'dew', 'pew', 'new' and write the words in a list under 'few'. Ask learners what they notice about the list and confirm that they all end in *ew* and they rhyme. Ensure that they know that if they can read and write 'few' they can read and write the other rhyming words as only the first sound(s) changes. Repeat the procedure for other words.

Suggested words: 'blew', 'crew', 'drew', 'flew', 'grew', 'screw', 'chew', 'threw'.

PCM 8 provides reinforcement of this sound.

Dictation
Use these or similar sentences to test spelling of words with the *ew* sound.

- A few girls came to tea.
- I have a new coat.
- The wind blew my hat away.
- The crew are on the ship.
- The dog likes to chew the bone.
- The new plants grew well.

Give learners practice in identifying where they hear the long vowel sound u in words, and how it is written when it is in the middle and when it is at the end of words.

Each learner will need: a piece of card/paper with *oo* written on it, a piece of card with *ew* written on it, or a mini-whiteboard and marker.

1 They point to/hold up the card or piece of paper with the letters *oo* or *ew* representing the sound written on it, when you say a word.

2 They should write *oo* or *ew* when you say a word.

Suggested words: 'broom', 'stew', 'flew', 'stool', 'mood', 'spoon', 'chew', 'threw', 'room', 'zoom', 'cool', 'crew', 'few', 'stoop', 'broom'.

Another less common representation of the long vowel *u* is *u–e*.

Write the words 'cube', 'mule', 'tube' and 'rule' on the whiteboard and ask the learners what they notice about the words. For example,

there are two pairs of rhyming words – 'cube'/'tube', 'mule'/'rule'.

Tell learners that when *e* comes at the end of a word, as in 'cube', the vowel in the middle says its name and not its sound, and the *e* at the end is silent.

Show examples of this, for example: 'cub' – 'cube'; 'tub' – 'tube'; 'cut' – 'cute'; 'us' – 'use'.

Tell learners that you want to write the word 'cube' and ask them how many sounds they can hear in the word 'cube'. Confirm three, *c-u-b* with a silent *e* at the end – 'cube' – and write 'cube' on the board. Remind learners that the *e* must go at the end to make the vowel long (it says its name and not its sound).

Repeat for the word 'tube'.

The following words should be learnt: 'cube', 'tube', 'mule', 'rule', 'use', 'fuse', 'June', 'tune', 'prune', 'cute', 'flute' and 'jute'.

PCM 9 can be used to reinforce the long *u* sound.

Dictation
These sentences are suitable for dictation in this unit.

- He has a tube of green paint.
- A cube has six sides.
- Tara can play the flute.
- June is the month after May.
- A prune is a dried plum.

Give learners the opportunity to practise auditory discrimination by checking if they can accurately identify short vowels and long vowels in words.

Say words and invite learners to answer 'short vowel' or 'long vowel'.

Examples: 'pup', 'prune', 'flume', 'fuss', 'duke', 'huff', 'cut', 'cube', 'June', 'but', 'tug', 'plume', 'fuse', 'mud', 'rude'.

The activities give practice in the different ways the long vowel is written in words like 'grew', 'tube', 'blue' and 'moon', i.e. *ew*, 'u–e', 'ue' and 'oo'.

1 Learners are asked to write the words for given pictures.

2 Learners are asked to write words with the long vowel *u* from a selection of words, some with short vowels and some with long vowels.

3 Learners are asked to use clues to work out words with the long vowel sound u in them.

Weekly review

Use this rubric to assess learners' progress as they worked through the activities this week.

Level	Reading	Writing
■	This group use phonics as the main method of tackling unfamiliar words and with some support are becoming more confident at recognising the different representations of the long vowels *e* and *u*.	This group can spell words with the different representations of the long vowels *e* and *u* when the words are in lists with the same spelling pattern. They are making good progress at choosing the correct representation when mixed lists are dictated.
●	This group use phonics as the main method of tackling unfamiliar words and recognise the different representations of the long vowels *e* and *u* most of the time.	This group can spell words with the different representations of the long vowels *e* and *u* and apply their knowledge of phonemes and spelling patterns in writing most of the time.
▲	This group use phonics as the main method of tackling unfamiliar words and recognise the different representations of the long vowels *e* and *u*.	This group can spell words with the different representations of the long vowels *e* and *u* and apply their knowledge of phonemes and spelling patterns in writing.

Week 3

Student's Book pages 17–20

Workbook pages 14–16

Workbook pages 14–15

Reading and writing

Talk about the shortened form of the countries' names – many being the first three letters as in Canada (CAN) but not all, e.g. China (CHN).

Extension: Learners research the shortened form where it is not the first three letters of the name, for example: China (CHN), Japan (JPN).

1 Learners are asked to match the shortened form to the full name of the country.

Before turning to Activities 2 and 3, ask learners what they understand by the term 'alphabetical order'. They may suggest class lists or the class register. Establish the understanding of alphabetical order by asking a number of learners to stand in line according to the first letter of their name. At this point choose only one name for each letter of the alphabet, but repeat so all learners have an opportunity to take part.

2 Ask learners to put names of countries in alphabetical order. Remind them that names of countries must have capital letters.

3 Ask learners to put names of sports in alphabetical order.

Answers
1 Jam – Jamaica; USA – United States of America; Eth – Ethiopia; Ken – Kenya; GBR – Great Britain
2 Australia, Brazil, China, Ethiopia, France, Italy, Japan, Mexico
3 badminton, cycling, football, gymnastics, hockey, judo, sailing

Student's Book pages 17–18

Reading

Give the learners the opportunity to look at and 'read' the table on page 17. Remind them that they don't need to read a table like this word for word. They should read the headings and familiarise themselves with what the chart is about.

Ask learners to read the chart by pointing to/answering questions such as:

- Show where you will find out about the winners of the Men's 5000 metres.
- Show where you will find out about the women's 100 metres hurdles.
- Who won the men's 100 metres?
- Who got a bronze medal in the women's 100 metres?
- What country got two gold medals?

When learners are comfortable reading the chart they should turn to the activities on page 18.

1 Learners write the names of the countries for each flag. The Olympic medal winner's table can be used as a reference.

2 The learners find answers to questions by reading the table.

Support: Support individuals or small groups to find the answers to the questions in the chart. The use of a 'marker' might be helpful for some learners. This will help to hold the place where the answer is while they write.

Answers
2 Sally Pearson; Dawn Harper; Aries Merritt, Jason Richardson, Hansle Parchment; Usain Bolt; men's 5000 metres; women's hundred metre hurdles; Tirunesh Dibaba Kenene.

Student's Book page 19
Reading and writing
Here, an extract has been taken from the previous table (women's 100 metre hurdles) and times have been added to it. The times are in seconds and learners could be given the opportunity to see what they can do in 12 seconds. For example: How far can they run? Not far! How many times can they bounce a ball? How far can they count up to?

1 The learners read the table and answer questions. Spend some time ensuring that the learners know how to read the table by asking questions such as:

- Who won the bronze medal?
- What country did the gold medallist come from?
- What country won two medals?
- What was the bronze medallist's time?

Support: The use of a 'marker' would be helpful here.

2 Before learners write their diary entry, take time to discuss things that they might write, how they would have felt, and build up a word bank with them. Learners then use these when planning their writing.

Answers
1 Sally Pearson; 12.35 seconds; Dawn Harper; USA.

Student's Book page 20
Reading and writing
1 Read the information about Usain Bolt with the learners and discuss the content before they answer the questions in activity 1.

2 Here the learners are asked to write a short story for the local newspaper about Usain Bolt's win at the 2012 Olympics.

Discuss the purpose of headlines and the format that they take. Have some examples of local newspapers showing headings. Invite learners to suggest examples of headlines for their stories about Usain Bolt. Write the suggestions on the whiteboard and discuss what is good about some and how others could be made better.

Discuss the key points that would be in an article about Usain Bolt's win and an opening sentence. Model writing an opening sentence.

Give the learners time to plan their article before writing.

Support: Some learners could work in pairs to plan their story. Support where necessary by helping them to focus on what would be important to include in the short article.

Answers
1 21 August 1986; Jamaica; Lightning Bolt; three; three.

Workbook pages 15–16
Reading
Learners are asked to read and follow instructions to make Olympic medals.

Ask learners to read 'What you need' and the 'Instructions' before organising the class in the way you would like them to work.

Check that they know what is needed and where they will find the materials.

Discuss the order of the instructions and how important it is to follow the order. Discuss whether it might be a good idea to paint the lids one day and leave them to dry before decorating.

Later, organise the learners to make Olympic rings, flags or torches for display. Discuss the materials that will be used and demonstrate how the rings/flags/torches are made. Describe what you are doing as you progress through each part of the activity.

Invite learners to retell the sequence of steps for making Olympic rings before making their own.

Based on their experience of making Olympic rings the learners should then write about how to make Olympic rings, flags or torches. They should use PCM 10 to record their work..

Weekly review

Use this rubric to assess learners' progress as they worked through the activities this week.

Level	Reading	Writing
■	This group can read and follow simple instructions with teacher support.	This group need support with organisational devices in non-fiction writing such as posters and newspaper stories.
●	This group can read and follow simple instructions with minimal support.	With minimal support this group can use organisational devices in non-fiction writing such as posters and newspaper stories.
▲	This group can read and follow simple instructions independently.	This group can use organisational devices in non-fiction writing such as posters and newspaper stories.

End of unit assessment

Use PCM 11 to recap work done in this unit and to assess whether learners are able to use the features of a known text (tables) to find information and answer questions. Let learners work independently to complete the task and then collect and check their answers.

Unit 3 What's for lunch?

Unit overview

As learners work through the unit they will have the opportunity to read and act out a story using different voices for characters, becoming aware of character and dialogue. They will have opportunities to retell and talk about events and characters in the story.

Worm Looks for Lunch is a play script.

The unit could be part of Science: plants and animals.

Learners will have opportunities to learn the different common spellings of long vowels.

Reading	Writing	Listening and speaking
2R02 Use phonics as the main method of tackling unfamiliar words; 2R06 Read aloud with increased accuracy, fluency and expression; 2R07 Begin to read with fluency and expression, taking some notice of punctuation, including speech marks; 2Ri2 Identify and describe story settings and characters, recognising that they may be from different times and places; 2R10 Discuss the meaning of unfamiliar words encountered in reading; 2Rx3 Find answers to questions by reading a section of text; 2Ri3 Make simple inferences from the words on the page, e.g. about feelings; 2R09 Locate words by initial letter in simple dictionaries, glossaries and indexes; 2Rv1 Show some awareness that texts have different purposes	2W04 Use simple non-fiction texts as a model for writing; 2W07 Make simple notes from a selection of non-fiction texts, e.g. listing key words; 2Wa2 Choose interesting words and phrases, e.g. in describing people and places; 2Wa3 Build and use collections of interesting and significant words; 2Wp1 Write in clear sentences using capital letters, full stops and question marks; 2Wa5 Use features of chosen text type; 2Wt1 Structure a story with a beginning, middle and end; 2Wt2 Use the language of time, e.g. 'suddenly', 'after that'; 2Wp3 Use mainly simple and compound sentences, with and/but to connect ideas; 'because' may begin to be used in a complex sentence; 2Ws1 Learn the different common spellings of long vowel phonemes; 2Ws2 Apply knowledge of phonemes and spelling patterns in writing independently as well as when writing sentences from memory dictated by the teacher from memory; 2Ws3 Secure the spelling of high frequency words and common irregular words	2SL5 Show awareness of the listener by including relevant details; 2SL6 Attempt to express ideas precisely, using a growing vocabulary; 2SL8 Demonstrate 'attentive listening' and engage with another speaker; 2SL10 Begin to be aware of ways in which speakers vary talk, e.g. the use of more formal vocabulary and tone of voice; 2SL11 Show awareness that speakers use a variety of ways of speaking in different situations and try out different ways of speaking

Related resources

- Slideshow 3: What's for lunch?
- Audio files: *Worm Looks for Lunch*; *Caterpillar*; *The Caterpillar*
- PCM 12: Food dictionary
- PCM 13: Phonics *ow* and *ou*
- PCM 14: End of unit assessment

Introducing the unit

Use photos of different natural foods (plant and animal based), to introduce the idea that different animals eat different kinds of food. Go through the photos and ask learners to identify the type of food and then to say what type/s of animals eat each kind of food.

Display the name of an animal, for example, parrot. Ask learners which of these foods a parrot would eat. Discuss other birds and what they eat, for example: herons and eagles eat fish, sunbirds eat nectar from flowers, and finches eat seeds and nuts. Repeat this for a few different animals as long as the learners maintain interest.

Tell the learners that in this unit they are going to learn more about what animals eat.

Week 1

Student's Book pages 21–25

Workbook page 17

Student's Book pages 21–24

Explain that *Worm Looks for Lunch* is a play. Ask learners to look through the pages and to say how they can tell this is a play, for example: the way the text is presented, stage directions, and so on.

Ask learners what they already know about plays. Are they read like story books or non-fiction books?

Give learners some time to look at the pictures and discuss the questions on page 21 before you begin to read the play.

Play the audio file for the learners. Allow them to work out who is talking in each scene based on the written text and the different voices. If you do not have access to this, read the play aloud, with expression and using different voices for each character.

Divide the learners into groups of six and give each learner a part to play.

Point out their character's name and the colour it is printed in. Draw their attention to capital letters, full stops, question marks and exclamation marks that may help in their reading. What do they notice about the style of writing? (Short, often repetitive sentences.)

Next, ask the groups to run through a draft reading, helping them if they struggle with unfamiliar words.

Draw the groups together as a class and read the play together. Encourage the learners to read with expression and praise self-correction and fluency.

Take the opportunity to highlight the word 'bark' (page 6), discuss its meaning in this context, and relate to 'park' and other *ar* words (Unit 1).

Student's Book page 25

Reading and writing

1 The learners are asked to write a list of the names of the characters in the play.

2 Before learners turn to this activity, discuss with them how the text is written in a different way from the text of a story, where people are speaking. There are no speech marks. Use *Jodie the Juggler* as an example of speech marks in text.

The learners then complete the activity using the text for reference.

3 Before turning to the activity, discuss with the learners when it is best to use 'and' to join two sentences, and when to use 'but' to join two sentences.

For example:

I like eating apples. I like eating peaches.

I like eating apples **and** I like eating peaches.

I like eating peaches. I don't like eating bananas.

I like eating peaches **but** I don't like eating bananas.

Answers
1 Worm, Storyteller, Rabbit, Deer, Beetle, Bird
2 Rabbit – "I like eating grass."
Bird – "I like eating beetles."
Worm – "I'm fed up with earth for lunch!"
Deer – "I like eating bark."
Beetle – "I like eating leaves."
Bird – "I like eating … WORMS!"
3 and, but, and, but

Workbook page 17

Reading

Before turning to the activity, ask the learners to scan the text and identify questions. Make sure they can find:

- Who are you?
- And what do you like to eat?

- You won't? Why not?
- What's that?

Discuss with the learners how they can recognise a question in text (by the use of a question mark). Draw the learners' attention to the question marks in the text.

Give learners some time to work in pairs, taking turns to ask a question and give an answer. Draw the class together and invite pairs to say their question/answer and invite their peers to identify the question and the answer. Ask learners if they notice any difference in the way a question is asked compared with how the answer is given (the tone of voice used for a question).

Answers
beetles/leaves; bird/beetles and worms; rabbit/grass; deer/bark

Weekly review

Use this rubric to assess learners' progress as they worked through the activities this week.

Level	Reading	Writing
■	This group read aloud with expression when taking on the role of a character in a play, once the text becomes familiar.	This group can use 'and' and 'but' to join two sentences.
●	This group read aloud with expression when taking on the role of a character in a play.	This group can use 'and' and 'but' to join two sentences. They are beginning to use them in their own writing.
▲	This group read aloud with fluency and expression when taking on the role of a character in a play.	This group understand and can use 'and' and 'but' to join two sentences. They use them when writing independently.

Week 2

Student's Book pages 26–27

Workbook pages 18–19

Student's Book page 26

Reading and writing

1 Learners are asked to write sentences to say why the worm didn't like eating grass, bark and leaves. Remind learners about the use of capital letters and full stops.

The focus of the rest of the activities moves to food that the learners like/dislike.

2 Learners are asked to write a list of things that they like to eat. Remind them how a list is written and demonstrate writing a list on the whiteboard, for example: a list of fruit, a list of girl's names, a list of the days of the week.

3–4 Learners draw a picture of themselves eating their favourite food before writing a caption under it.

5–6 Before turning to these activities, discuss with the learners why they like/dislike certain foods and elicit words that are used to describe food, such as 'yummy', 'delicious', 'tasty', 'scrumptious', 'juicy', 'dry', 'spicy', 'yuck', 'sweet', 'bitter', 'sour', 'crunchy', 'chewy', 'salty', 'sweet'.

Answers
1 it was too chewy; it was too hard; it was too dry

Take the opportunity at this time to do some further work on alphabetical order with the learners. Using lists of fruit such as kiwi, melon, pineapple, lychee, banana, fig; or vegetables such as asparagus, mushroom, potato, okra, zucchini, the learners write the names of the fruit or vegetables in alphabetical order.

PCM 12 gives the learners the opportunity to write a food dictionary. They find and write the meanings of five food words.

Student's Book page 27

Reading and writing

1 In this activity learners are asked to use words (adjectives) that can be used to describe food, in order to copy and complete sentences.

Before turning to the activity ask the learners to identify the adjectives in phrases, for example: 'a juicy peach',' a crunchy apple', 'a bitter lemon'. Discuss the purpose of the adjective and how adjectives can make writing more interesting.

Invite learners to supply adjectives to describe words, for example: 'sky', 'day', 'water', 'vegetables', 'chocolate', 'car', 'chair', 'sea', 'flowers', 'toffee', 'mountains'.

The activity asks the learners to choose the correct adjectives to complete sentences about food.

2 The learners write their own sentences with the adjectives 'delicious' and 'tasty'.

3 In this activity, learners are asked to write sentences about food that they don't like, giving the reason why.

Model sentences to show the use of 'because'. For example:

- I don't like chocolate because it melts too easily.
- I don't like potatoes because they are too dry.

4 Learners are asked to design a box for a new cereal. They should think about the size and style of the lettering, the artwork and perhaps a slogan that might make people want to eat the new cereal. This is a good opportunity for the learners to form letters correctly in a different context. Have some cereal boxes for them to look at and discuss which ones they think are good and why.

Answers
1 hard, bitter, juicy, sticky, sweet, crunchy

Workbook page 18
Writing
Before turning to this activity, discuss with the learners where they might eat other than at home. Discuss menus and what might be on a menu. Discuss the style of writing that might be used and any artwork. Discuss names of cafés and why they might have been chosen, for example, the owner's name, association with where they are situated or what they sell: The Sea View; Coffee House; Aloo Palace.

Workbook page 19
Sounds and spelling
Before turning to the activity, focus on the different representations of the long vowel sound *i*.

Learners will already know that the long vowel sound *i* can be represented by *igh*. Tell the learners that the long vowel sound *i* can be represented in different ways.

Ask learners to read the text on page 3 of the play script and identify a word with the long vowel sound *i* ('try').

Tell learners that the long vowel sound *i* in the middle of a word is usually represented by *igh* and at the end of a word by *y*.

Exceptions: 'high', 'sigh', 'thigh', 'die', 'lie', 'pie', 'tie'.

Learners will be familiar with words like 'my' and 'by' as high frequency words, and should learn to spell 'cry', 'dry', 'fry', 'try', 'fly', 'sly', 'sky', 'sty', 'spy', 'why'.

Give learners some practice in identifying where they hear the long vowel sound *i* in words, and how it is written when it is in the middle and when it is at the end of words.

Each learner will need: a piece of card/paper with *igh* written on it; a piece of card with *y* written on it; or a mini-whiteboard and marker.

1 Learners point to/hold up the correct card or piece of paper with the letters representing the long vowel sound *i*, *igh* or *y* written on it when the teacher says a word.

2 Learners should write *igh* or *y* when the teacher says a word.

Suggested words: 'night', 'shy', 'cry', 'tight', 'bright', 'light', 'why', 'by', 'flight', 'fly', 'fright', 'my', 'try', 'might', 'right', 'sky'.

Give learners the opportunity to practise the 'join' of *igh*. This reinforces that the letters make one sound.

Learners should use the 'joins' when writing the words.

Support: Support individuals or small groups as necessary when dictating words for spelling by saying things like: Where do you hear the sound? Is it at the beginning or at the end? What letters should we write?

Dictation
These sentences, or similar ones, can be used for dictation to test spelling in this unit.

- A fly is on the cake.
- We will fry the fish to eat.
- I might go to the park today.
- The class will try to sing the song.
- The night sky is dark.

Another representation of the long vowel *i* is *i–e*. The word 'like' appears in a number of places in the text and the learners will know this word as a high frequency word.

Ask learners to work first on their own and then in pairs to count the number of times the word 'like' appears in the play (13 times).

Tell learners that when e comes at the end of a word, as in 'like', the vowel in the middle says its name and not its sound, and the e at the end is silent.

There are many examples which show how adding an e at the end makes the short vowel long. Show examples of this: 'pip' – 'pipe'; 'rip' – 'ripe'; 'din' – 'dine'; 'fin' – 'fine'; 'bit' – 'bite'; 'pin' – 'pine'; 'win' – 'wine'; 'twin' – 'twine'; 'shin' – 'shine'; 'kit' – 'kite'; 'hid' – 'hide'.

Tell learners that you want to write the word 'pipe' and ask them how many sounds they can hear in the word 'pipe'. Confirm three – p-i-p with a silent e at the end – 'pipe', and write 'pipe' on the board. Remind learners that the e must go at the end to make the vowel long (it says its name and not its sound).

Repeat for the words 'ripe', 'wipe', 'swipe'.

The following words should be learnt: 'hide', 'ride', 'tide', 'side', 'wide', 'slide', 'bride'; 'dine', 'fine', 'line', 'mine', 'nine', 'pine', 'wine', 'twine', 'shine'; 'mime', 'time', 'chime'; 'file', 'pile', 'tile', 'smile', 'while'; 'bite', 'kite', 'white'; 'like', 'bike', 'hike', 'trike'.

Dictation

i–e

The plum is ripe.

The tile fell off the roof.

Mike can ride his bike.

I got white sheets for the bed.

I like green grapes.

igh, y, ie

Last night we saw the moon in the sky.

I lost my tie.

Why did you fight with him?

My bike has a bright light.

The white cloth is dry.

Extension: Learners should learn to spell and use correctly words like 'I'/'eye' and 'by'/'bye'/'buy'.

Note: The words in each group sound the same but have different spellings and are called 'homophones'.

Answers
1 tie, fly, nine, light
2 Learners' own answers.
3 Learners' own answers.

Weekly review

Use this rubric to assess learners' progress as they worked through the activities this week.

Level	Reading	Writing
■	This group use phonics as the main method of tackling unfamiliar words. They are becoming quicker and more accurate at doing so. They recognise the different representations of the long vowel sound *i*.	This group can spell words with the different representations of the long vowels *a, o, e, u* and *i* and are becoming more able to do this when the words are not in lists with like representations of a sound.
●	This group use phonics as the main method of tackling unfamiliar words and recognise the different representations of the long vowel sound *i*.	This group can spell words with the different representations of the long vowels *a, o, e, u* and *i*. They can apply their knowledge most of the time in their independent writing.
▲	This group use phonics as the main method of tackling unfamiliar words and recognise the different representations of the long vowel sound *i* reading words with speed and accuracy.	This group can spell words with the different representations of the long vowels *a, o, e, u*, and *i*. They apply their knowledge in their independent writing.

Week 3

Student's Book pages 28–31

Workbook pages 20–22

Student's Book page 28

Writing

1–2 In these activities learners are asked to list the characters in the order that the worm met them, and then beside each character's name write what it ate.

3 In this activity learners are asked to work in pairs and take turns at imagining that he or she is the worm telling its story.

Before setting the learners to do this, model what the worm might have said when he was telling what happened.

For example: 'Yesterday, when I went looking for food I met a rabbit. He was munching some grass. I tried to eat some grass. I didn't like it because it was too chewy.'

'Next I met a deer. He was standing under a tree eating the bark. I tried to eat the bark but I didn't like it. It was too hard.'

Note: This is an opportunity to further develop the use of conjunctions in writing.

4 Before the learners write the story, talk about the language of time that helps to show the order of events in a story, for example: 'then', 'next', 'lastly' or 'last of all'.

A framework using these words and artwork showing the order in which the worm met the characters is given.

Answers
1 Rabbit, Deer, Beetle, Bird
2 Rabbit – grass; Deer – bark; Beetle – leaves; Bird – beetles and worms

Workbook page 20

Sounds and spelling

The activities in this section focus on *ou* and *ow* making the same sound. Give the learners opportunities to hear and identify the sound represented by *ou* in words.

Say a word like 'loud' and ask learners how many sounds they can hear in the word 'loud' and confirm three – *l-ou-d*. Write the word 'loud' and highlight the *ou* representing the middle sound.

Write the words 'found', 'hound', 'round', 'sound', 'pound' and 'ground' in a list on the whiteboard. Ask learners what they notice about the words in the list. Confirm that they all have *ou* in the middle, *nd* at the end, and that the words all rhyme. Ensure that the learners know that if they can read and write 'found' they can read and write all the other words as only the first letter(s) changes.

Suggested words to read and spell: 'mouth', 'south', 'mouse', 'house', 'trout', 'spout', 'shout', 'grout', 'snout', 'stout', 'scout', 'loud', 'cloud', 'proud', 'count', 'mount'.

Give learners practice in writing the letter join *ou*. The learners should write *ou* words to dictation. This will reinforce letter sequence and motor memory.

Give learners similar opportunities to investigate *ow*, as in 'how'.

(Learners will have learnt about the letters *ow* making the long vowel sound *o* previously.)

Words to investigate: 'cow', 'how', 'now', 'row', 'bow', 'town', 'down', 'gown', 'frown', 'drown', 'brown', 'owl', 'howl', 'fowl', 'growl', 'towel', 'vowel', 'tower', 'power', 'flower', 'shower'.

Give learners some practice in writing the letter strings until they become automatic: *–own, –ower, –ound, –out, –oud, –ouse, –ount, –outh*.

Note: A letter string is a sequence of letters that occur frequently.

It is not easy to know when to use *ou* and when to use *ow*.

Ou and *ow* are both used in the middle of words, but *ou* is never used at the end of a word – always use *ow* (except for older words like 'thou'). It is usually correct to use *ou* before *t* ('shou'), *se* ('mouse'), *th* ('south'), *nd* ('round'), *nt* ('count').

1 In this activity, learners are asked to write words for pictures. The words have the sound represented by *ou* in the middle.

2 Learners are asked to write rhyming words ending in *–ouse, –oud, –outh, –out*.

3–4 These are similar to Activities 1 and 2 but with *ow* as the focus.

PCM 13 gives additional practice in spelling words with the *ow* or *ou* sound.

Dictation
- The towel is on the shelf.
- The mouse ran to the hole.
- The owl flew round the tree.
- We get milk from a cow.
- The house has a brown roof.

Extension: Able learners could investigate:

1 the different pronunciations of *ow* in words like 'bow', 'sow' and 'row'

2 homophones such as 'flower'/'flour', 'fowl'/'foul'.

Answers
1 mouse, mouth, cloud
2 Learners' own answers.
3 owl, cow, crown
4 Learners' own answers.

Student's Book page 29

Reading, speaking and listening

1–2 Introduce the word 'caterpillar' to the class and then ask them to read the two poems on their own. Give them some time to do this before letting them discuss and explain their preferences.

Both poems are short and could be memorised for a class recitation.

Writing

1 The list of words used to describe caterpillars is a good place to focus on handwriting skills and the joining of letters. If there is time, let learners make illustrated and coloured lists.

2 Learners find the rhyming words.

Answers
Activity 2
1 Learners' own answers.
2 down/brown; furry/hurry; walk/stalk; day/away

Student's Book page 30

Spelling

1 Before turning to the activities, refer learners back to *Worm Looks for Lunch* and ask them to find examples of the words 'to' and 'too' in the text.

Examples: "And what do you like to eat?"

"It's too chewy/hard/dry."

Elicit from the learners their different usage and spellings.

Elicit from the learners the other spelling, i.e. 'two'.

Give learners practice in selecting the correct spelling, ensuring that they know that the surrounding text will determine the spelling, i.e. 'to', 'too' or 'two'. For example, write some sentences on the whiteboard with 'to', 'too' and

'two' missed out, and ask learners to say which one to use.

I have _____ hands.

The water is _____ cold to swim in.

I went _____ my friend's house.

It was _____ hot _____ play outside.

Note: Question 2 recaps on the three representations of the long vowel sound *a* with the words 'snails', 'trays', 'cakes'.

Answers
1 too, to, to, too, too
2 two flags, two snails, two trays, two cakes
3 too, two, to, too, to, two

Workbook page 21

Writing

Before asking learners to write, elicit from them how the bird's story might differ from the worm's story. What kind of character was the bird compared with the worm? How do the learners think the bird felt about the worm?

Talk about the three pictures on page 21, which will help learners plan a beginning, a middle and an end for their story.

Before setting the learners to do this, model with them what the bird might have said when he was telling what happened. For example: 'One day I was looking for some food when I met a silly little worm. He wriggled right up to me and asked *me* what I liked to eat!'

Student's Book page 31

Reading and writing

1–3 Before learners work at these activities, draw them together and discuss, plan and prepare for a performance of *Worm Looks for Lunch*. Talk about costumes, tickets, programmes, advertising posters, the cast, rehearsals, performance and an audience.

4 Learners put the instructions for putting on a play into the correct sequence.

Answers
1 ticket, programme, poster, costume
4 Choose the people to be each character.; Rehearse the play.; Put on the costumes.; Perform the play.

Workbook page 22

Writing

The last activity in this unit asks the learners to complete audience speech bubbles with comments about the play. Discuss with them what members of the audience might say after watching a play, for example: 'I really enjoyed that.', 'I could hear every word.', 'The costumes were very good.' Also discuss what some members of an audience might say that would help make the next performance better such as, 'I couldn't see everybody on the stage.'

Model writing what the audience might say after they had enjoyed the performance.

Weekly review

Use this rubric to assess learners' progress as they worked through the activities this week.

Level	Writing
■	This group can tell a story with a beginning, a middle and an end. With support they can then write the story.
●	This group can write a short story with a beginning, a middle and an end. They are beginning to write a variety of sentence types and use interesting vocabulary.
▲	This group can write a short story with a beginning, a middle and an end. They write with a variety of sentence types and use interesting vocabulary.

End of unit assessment

Use PCM 14 as an additional vocabulary task for this unit. Let learners complete it in class or as homework. Check the answers as a class, allowing learners to assess their own work based on the given answers.

Unit 4 Kind Emma

Unit overview

The story in this unit is *Kind Emma*, a fairy-tale narrative with a familiar setting. The theme of the story is universal – kindness is its own reward.

As learners work through this unit they will develop their reading skills by reading with increased accuracy, fluency and expression, taking some notice of punctuation including speech marks. Text is presented in larger blocks, encouraging learners to read with less reliance on visual cues.

Learners will have opportunities to develop their understanding of text and to explore how writers structure text and use language features, including the language of time. They will develop their ability to express their likes and dislikes in reading.

The activities provide opportunities to develop writing skills further, taking account of punctuation and increased use of accurate spelling

Reading	Writing	Listening and speaking
2R06 Read aloud with increased accuracy, fluency and expression;	2W03 Begin to reread own writing aloud to check for sense and accuracy;	2SL1 Recount experiences and explore possibilities;
2R07 Begin to read with fluency and expression, taking some notice of punctuation, including speech marks;	2W05 Use the structures of familiar poems and stories in developing own writing;	2SL2 Explain plans and ideas, extending them in the light of discussion;
2R10 Discuss the meaning of unfamiliar words encountered in reading;	2W06 Plan writing through discussion or by speaking aloud;	2SL3 Articulate clearly so that others can hear;
2Rx1 Read and respond to question words, e.g. 'what', 'where', 'when', 'who', 'why';	2Wa4 Begin to use dialogue in stories; 2Wa7 Write simple evaluations of books read;	2SL6 Attempt to express ideas precisely, using a growing vocabulary;
2Rx3 Find answers to questions by reading a section of text;	2Wt1 Structure a story with a beginning, middle and end;	2SL7 Listen carefully and respond appropriately, asking questions of others;
2Ri1 Predict story endings;	2Wp1 Write in clear sentences using capital letters, full stops and question marks;	2SL8 Demonstrate 'attentive listening' and engage with another speaker
2Ri2 Identify and describe story settings and characters, recognising that they may be from different times and places;	2Wp3 Use mainly simple and compound sentences, with 'and'/'but' to connect ideas; 'because' may begin to be used in a complex sentence;	
2Ri3 Make simple inferences from the words on the page, e.g. about feelings;	2Wp4 Use past and present tenses accurately (if not always consistently);	
2Rw1 Comment on some vocabulary choices, e.g. adjectives;	2Ws1 Learn the different common spellings of long vowel phonemes;	
2Rw2 Talk about what happens at the beginning, in the middle or at the end of a story;	2Ws2 Apply knowledge of phonemes and spelling patterns in writing independently as well as when writing sentences from memory dictated by the teacher;	
	2Ws3 Secure the spelling of high frequency words and common irregular words;	
	2Ws4 Spell words with common prefixes and suffixes, e.g. *un–*, *dis–*, *–ful*, *–ly*.	

Related resources

- Slideshow 4: *Kind Emma*
- Audio file: *Kind Emma*
- PCM 15: Prefixes
- PCM 16: End of unit assessment

Introducing the unit

The concept of kindness is an important one for young children and there are many social benefits from introducing the idea of being kind in the classroom.

Begin by displaying the word 'kindness' in the centre of the whiteboard. Ask learners to say what the word means to them. Write their contributions and ideas around the central word. Allow for examples rather than definitions of kindness (sharing, nice words, helping people who have hurt themselves and so on). You may want to discuss who we need to be kind to (ourselves, other people, animals, the environment and so on).

Next, ask the learners: How are you kind at home and at school? Try to give everyone a chance to contribute something. If the class is too large to go around everyone, have learners tell the others in their groups one thing they do to be kind.

Give each learner a piece of coloured paper or card about A5 size. Tell them they are going to make a display entitled 'Kindness starts with me'. Ask them to draw a kindness portrait, showing themselves and what kindness means to them. Mount and display the portraits for the class (or as part of a larger school display).

World Kindness Day is celebrated by schools internationally on 13 November each year. See www.randomactsofkindness.org/world-kindness-day, or search the internet for posters, resources and teaching ideas around the theme of kindness, and for ideas and information.

Week 1

Student's Book pages 32–34

Workbook page 23

Student's Book pages 32–33

Tell learners that they are going to read a story about a person called Emma. Show them a picture of Emma and spend some time talking about what sort of person she might be. Ask the learners to give evidence from the picture to support their suggestions.

Tell the class that the story is called *Kind Emma*. Ask learners to predict what might happen in the story. Encourage them to give reasons for their answers.

Explain to the learners that some stories have unusual characters and this is one of them. Show the 'thing' (page 32) and ask them to predict what its role might be in the story.

Ask the learners to read the story quietly and independently. Monitor progress and ask individual learners to read aloud if necessary. Check that the learners are using a range of strategies to tackle unknown words: looking at the pictures, sounding out words, using context and grammatical clues, reading on and rereading.

For example, 'Goodnight!' (page 33) is a compound word. Breaking the word into its two component parts will help with reading.

Check:

- Can the learners 'see' the two smaller words within 'goodnight' – 'good' and 'night'?
- Can the learners recognise and read the common spellings of long vowels, for example, *oo* and *igh*?
- Can the learners blend the initial sound, the long vowel sound and the final sound to read the word – *g-oo-d* n-*igh-t*?
- Can the learners then read the whole word – 'goodnight'?

Support: During this time, work in small groups with any learners who need more direct support to help them apply the strategies.

Draw the class together and invite individuals to read while others follow the text. Highlight and praise strategies used to decipher any new or unfamiliar words. Spend as much time as necessary with individuals or groups to ensure accurate decoding.

Ask the learners to reread certain parts of the story and to comment on the punctuation. How does the punctuation help with expression when they read?

Spend time ensuring understanding of the text before moving on to the Workbook and Student's Book activities by asking questions, discussing and developing answers.

For example:

- Why was Emma lonely?

  Encourage learners to show the evidence in the text that supports their answer ('Kind Emma lived all alone with no one to talk to.').

- How do you know that the 'thing' was frightened?

  Again ask the learners to show the evidence for their answer. The illustrations depict this along with the text ('The tiny thing stayed hidden. It was afraid to come out.').

Workbook page 23

Reading and writing

This activity highlights some of the vocabulary from the story that will be used in the Student's Book page 34.

Learners are asked to write the correct word for each picture.

The words are out of context, and here the learners need to use the illustrations and phonic cues to read and match the words to the pictures for copying. Ask them to identify each picture to avoid any confusion as to what word they should write, for example, the image of the bowl of soup, where the word 'soup' is the word to be matched from the box. Learners are looking for a word beginning with s for 'soup' and not d for 'dish' or b for 'bowl'.

Answers
door, fire, soup, table, 'thing', bread, spoon, house

Student's Book page 34

Reading and writing

Discuss with the learners how the story of *Kind Emma* is written in the past tense. Remind them that the author is telling the story about something that already happened to Emma.

Invite learners to give examples of things they did in the past. Use sentence openers such as:

- Yesterday I …
- Last week I…

Ask learners to identify the verbs used, for example: 'walked', 'went', 'jumped', 'played'. Then, using the text, ask them to identify verbs in the past tense.

Examples: 'lived'; 'poked'; 'stayed'.

1–3 Before the learners complete Activities 1–3, focus on what they are asked to do in activity 3 – write a sentence using 'and' to tell what Emma did next.

Discuss what Emma did and how the two things could be joined by a conjunction.

For example: Emma said, "Goodnight"./She left the room./She went upstairs./She went to bed.

If the learners are able, spend some time discussing alternatives to 'and' for joining the sentences. For example: Emma said, "Goodnight" before she went upstairs. Or, Emma said, "Goodnight" when she left the room.

Extension: Able learners can spend some time finding examples in the text where the past tense is not used and discuss why it is not used.

Direct speech examples: "You can share what I have," said Kind Emma.

"Come into my house," said Kind Emma.

4–6 The focus is on the learners' homes – where they live and who they live with.

Before learners turn to this activity, invite them to give sentences orally. Model writing a variety of sentence types on the whiteboard and invite learners to improve the given sentences, for example: by adding adjectives, by checking that a capital letter and a full stop have been used.

Answers
1 Kind Emma, the 'thing'
2 lived, scuttled, poked, put, stayed, was

Weekly review

Use this rubric to assess learners' progress as they worked through the activities this week.

Level	Reading	Writing	Listening and speaking
■	This group read with increased accuracy but still need some support to decode unfamiliar words.	This group are beginning to use capital letters and full stops when writing in sentences.	At times this group needs support to listen and respond appropriately.
●	This group are beginning to read with increased accuracy, fluency and expression.	This group can write in clear sentences using capital letters and full stops. They are beginning to use the past and present tenses with some accuracy.	This group demonstrate attentive listening. They listen carefully and respond appropriately.
▲	This group read with increased accuracy, fluency and expression, taking some notice of punctuation including speech marks.	This group can write in clear sentences using capital letters and full stops. They can use the past and present tenses accurately.	This group demonstrate attentive listening and engage with another speaker. They listen carefully and respond appropriately.

Week 2

Student's Book pages 35–37

Workbook pages 24–27

Workbook page 24

Reading

Before turning to the activity, ask the learners to reread the story. Then invite them to tell the main points of the story in order.

For example:

- Emma lived alone.
- A 'thing' came to her house.
- The 'thing' was frightened.
- Emma gave the 'thing' soup.
- Emma went to bed.
- Next morning the house was tidy.
- The 'thing' stayed with Emma.

The activity asks the learners to match the beginning of sentences with their endings to tell the story.

Remind them to read and check that each sentence makes sense. They should refer back to the text if necessary.

Answers

Kind Emma lived all alone with no one to talk to.
One night, a little voice called, "Oh, dear Emma, oh!"

She opened the door and a tiny 'thing' scuttled in.
She put a dish of hot soup and a very small spoon on the table.
She hoped the tiny 'thing' would come out and eat if she left the room.
Next morning when Emma awoke … the fire burned and the water was hot.

Student's Book page 35

Reading and writing

This section focuses on the theme of kindness and what tells the reader that Emma was kind.

1–2 Before turning to Activities 1 and 2, ask the learners to give further examples of:

- when they were kind to someone at school
- when someone was kind to them at home.

Focus on how the learners know that Emma was kind. Ask them to support their answers by showing the evidence in the illustrations (facial expressions, gestures) and text.

Listening and speaking

Give learners time to work in pairs and talk about one kind thing they have done. Learners should remember to say who the person was that they were kind to (a friend, a family member, a stranger), the person's name and what the kind thing was that they did.

Invite a learner to tell their peers about the kind deed that he/she did. Invite others to

50

check if the learner has included the three points:

- the person's name
- who the person was – friend, relative, stranger
- what the kind deed was.

Invite others to tell about their kind deed and ask their peers to check if the three points have been included.

Writing

1–2 Remind learners that these are the three points to include in their stories:

- the person's name
- who the person was – friend, relative, stranger
- what the kind deed was.

Encourage learners to check their stories. Have they included the three points? Are there any spelling errors that they can correct?

Extension: Learners could make a display of kind deeds that they have done. They could each write a short statement telling about a kind thing that they did. For example:

- I washed the dishes.
- I tidied my room.
- I played with my sister.
- I shared my toys.

This is an ideal opportunity to focus on broad writing skills and letter formation. Ask learners to use different styles, sizes of letters and colours to make their display attractive so that it stands out.

Learners can illustrate by drawing or bringing a photograph from home of them doing a kind deed, for example, playing with their sister.

Workbook page 25

Sounds and spelling

1–4 This section focuses on the letter strings *or* and *er*. It is often difficult for learners to hear and identify vowels correctly when they are followed by *r*. Missing out the vowel or writing the wrong vowel is a common error in writing words where the vowel is followed by *r*. This is a good time to remind learners that all words must have a vowel (or the letter *y*).

Revise the spelling pattern *ar* and invite learners to generate words with this spelling pattern. Give them a word to start say, such as 'car', and encourage them to use onset and rime to generate rhyming words, for example: 'car', 'bar', 'jar', 'far', 'tar'.

Use 'ark' and 'card' as start words.

Investigate the spelling pattern *–er* in words like 'her', 'herd', 'fern', 'term'.

The letter string *–er* appears at the end of some words like 'moth*er*', 'fath*er*', 'broth*er*', 'sist*er*', 'silv*er*', and as the comparative form of words like 'winn*er*', 'thinn*er*', 'bigg*er*', 'hard*er*', 'soft*er*'.

Investigate the spelling pattern *–or* in words – 'f*or*k', 'c*or*k', 'h*or*n', 'b*or*n', 'sh*or*t', 'st*or*k'.

Give learners three pieces of paper and ask them to write *ar* on one, *er* on another and *or* on the third.

Say words aloud and invite learners to hold up/point to the piece of paper that represents the vowel + *r* sound in the words that you say.

An alternative way is to ask the learners to write on mini-whiteboards the letters that represent the sound (*–ar*, *–er*, *–or*) that they hear in the words that you say.

Suggested words: 'park', 'short', 'charm', 'cord', 'her', 'fern', 'horn', 'sharp', 'term', 'lord'.

The learners should practise the joins *–ar*, *–er* and *–or* in handwriting.

Dictation

These sentences can be used throughout the week for dictation to reinforce spelling rules and listening skills.

- The car is in the car park.
- I sent him a card.
- The stem has a thorn on it.
- The stork has long legs.
- She took her books home.
- My sister stood at the kerb.

Answers

1 corn, horn, born; cork, stork
2 born, horn, torn, thorn
3 n, j, q, s,
4 shower, brother, sister, flower, winner, silver

Workbook page 26

Reading and writing

1–3 This section gives further practice in identifying verbs, choosing the correct verb to complete sentences and using a verb in a sentence. Before turning to the activities, give learners opportunities to identify verbs in spoken sentences.

Examples: I opened the door.

He went to the shops.

The girl ran home.

Student's Book page 36

Reading and writing
1 Learners are asked to make two lists: one of things that Emma did and one of things that the 'thing' did.

Show how the learners should write a heading for each list. For example:

Things Emma did   Things the 'thing' did
2 Learners write the verbs from activity 1.
3 Learners match verbs to words with a similar meaning.

Student's Book page 37

Reading and writing
1 This activity develops the concepts of true and false and introduces the idea that sometimes you 'can't tell' whether something is true or false using only the given information.

Use sentences like the ones below to establish that although these things might be true there is no evidence in the text to tell the learner that they are true.

- Emma has two beds in the house.
- Emma likes dancing.
- Emma painted the door red.

Remind the learners that they must be able to find evidence in the text or in the pictures in this unit to be able to say that something is true or false.

Give oral examples to check understanding of 'true', 'false' and can't tell'.

For example:

- Emma lived in a house.
- Emma lived with her brother.
- Emma used to live with her brother.
- Emma shared her soup.

- Emma liked to make soup.
- Emma finished all the soup.

2 This activity asks the learners to use words with prefixes to complete sentences.

Workbook page 27

Reading and writing
1–2 These activities focus on prefixes. A prefix is a group of letters at the beginning of a word. Write some words on the whiteboard and look at some similarities and differences in each pair of words.

- 'pack'/'unpack'
- 'lock'/'unlock'
- 'happy'/'unhappy'
- 'zip'/'unzip'

Ask learners to highlight the part of each word that makes it different from its partner. Elicit from them what adding *un*– before a word has done to the meaning of the word.

Establish with the learners that:

- *un*– is a prefix
- a prefix is a letter or group of letters added to the beginning of a word to make a new word
- when *un*– is added to the beginning of many words it gives the word the opposite meaning, for example, 'able'/'*un*able'.

Challenge the learners to think of as many words as they can that begin with the prefix *un*–. Write the given words with the prefix *un*– on the whiteboard.

Give learners practice in writing words with the prefix *un*–.

Suggested words: 'unhappy', 'unlucky', 'untie', 'unwell', 'untidy', 'unzip', 'unlock', 'unpack', 'unable'.

Note: Monitor where any errors might occur, with the prefix or with the root word.

The prefix *dis*– also makes the opposite of the word to which it is added.

Similar activities can be repeated for *dis*–.

Learners should then complete the activities on page 27.

Dictation

These, or similar sentences, can be used to reinforce use of words with the prefix *un–* or *dis–*.

- I was unwell last Sunday.
- He is unable to come next week.
- I had to unlock my case.
- The classroom is untidy.
- I dislike that smell.

Answers

1 unzip, unlock, dislike, unpack, disappear, disagree

2 zip, lock, like, pack, appear, agree

Extension: Investigate with the learners other common prefixes such as *re–*. Ask them to look at any posters/leaflets within the school about recycling. Discuss the meaning of the prefix *re–* (it means 'again'). Discuss the words 'refill' and 'reuse'.

Other words include: *re* + 'take'; *re* + 'visit'; *re* + 'play'; *re* + 'write'; *re* + 'tell'; *re* + 'place'; *re* + 'build'; *re* + 'heat'.

Learners could then turn to PCM 15 to practise using *un–*, *dis–* and *re–*.

Weekly review

Use this rubric to assess learners' progress as they worked through the activities this week.

Level	Reading	Writing	Listening and speaking
■	This group can find answers by reading a section of text. They need support to make simple inferences.	This group can write short texts with support to organise their ideas. They can spell many phonically regular words accurately.	This group enjoy recounting experiences but need some support to organise their thoughts.
●	This group can find answers by reading a section of text. At times they need some support to make simple inferences. They understand the concepts of true and false.	This group can write short texts independently, spelling most phonically regular words accurately.	This group can recount experiences and show some awareness of the listener.
▲	This group can find answers by reading a section of text. They can make simple inferences and understand the concepts of true and false.	This group can write short texts independently, spelling phonically regular words accurately.	This group can recount experiences speaking clearly and audibly.

Week 3

Student's Book pages 38–40

Workbook pages 28–29

Workbook page 28

Reading

Before learners turn to this activity ask them to reread the story. Discuss strategies for putting the sentences in order.

- Read all the sentences first before writing any numbers.

- Look for possible clues – is there a sentence that is obviously first? Think back to the story. What happened first? Similarly, is there a sentence that is obviously last?

- What had to happen to make something else happen? For example: Emma heard a little noise and so she opened the door.

- Look for words like 'then' and 'next'. These words mean that something else had to have happened before that part of the story.

- Read and reread. Is the order making sense? Check with the text if necessary.

Support: Support learners who need help by giving them copied versions of the page text. This will allow them to cut and manipulate the sentences to complete the task.

Student's Book page 38

Reading and writing

This activity helps develop the concept of time in stories and the language of time.

Ask learners to recite the days of the week in order before doing some 'quick-fire' questions such as:

- What day comes after Wednesday?
- What day comes before Saturday?
- Monday, Tuesday, Wednesday – What is the next day?

Discuss with learners what words and phrases can be used in stories to denote when something happened/will happen.

Examples: 'tomorrow', 'yesterday', 'today', 'next day', 'in a few days', 'last week', 'next week'.

Learners should choose one of the words/phrases and give an example of it used in a sentence.

Discuss words/phrases that can be used to denote the order of events that might happen on the same day.

Examples: 'firstly', 'next', 'after that', 'last of all', 'lastly', 'in the morning', 'when I got up', 'before lunch', 'after lunch'.

Again, learners should choose one of the words/phrases and give an example of it used in a sentence.

1 Learners write the names of the days of the week.

2 Learners copy sentences onto the correct page of a diary.

3 Learners draw five things, in sequence, that they do in a school day and write a caption for each picture.

Remind learners to use words that will help the reader to know the order in which things happened.

Answers
1 Monday, Tuesday, Wednesday, Thursday, Friday, Saturday, Sunday
2 Monday: I was lonely.; A thing 'thing' came into my house.; I gave it a dish of hot soup.; I said goodnight and went to bed.; I played 'snakes and ladders' with the 'thing'.

Tuesday: When I awoke the house was clean and tidy.; There was fresh bread on the table.; I had someone to talk to.
3 Learners' own answers.

Student's Book page 39

Reading and writing

1–2 The four pictures depict the main parts of the story from Emma opening the door to Emma going to bed. Using these as a guide, learners write the story to that point before writing what happened next.

3 Ask learners to work in pairs and talk about a different ending to the story: 'Next morning, when Emma awoke …'

Draw the class together and invite pairs to tell their ideas for a different ending.

4 The learners write a different ending to the story.

Support: Support individuals by scribing their story as they tell it. This allows learners who may have difficulty with handwriting, organisational skills, and/or spelling to create and tell their story.

Student's Book page 40

Writing

This activity focuses on learners using the structure of a simple story to plan and develop their own writing.

1 Learners talk about the main ideas, in sequence, of the story *Kind Emma*.

2 Learners are asked to use the same structure, to talk about and plan a story.

During discussion, learners should be encouraged to jot down key words and phrases for their later writing. Provide a planning sheet if appropriate.

Monitor carefully to ensure that learners are not spending time writing too much at this stage.

3 Learners write their own story.

Before learners turn to the activity, remind them of what you will be looking for in their stories. Discuss these with the learners and write them on the whiteboard.

Examples:
- Has the story a beginning, a middle and an ending?
- Are there capital letters at the beginning of sentences and full stops at the end?
- Have 'time' words been used?

Workbook page 29

Writing

Before learners write a book review discuss why people write book reviews and where they might find them.

Get some book reviews written by learners in another class to read to your class. Ask the learners if these book reviews would make them want to read the book. Why? Why not?

Invite learners to say why they liked or did not like *Kind Emma*, encouraging them to give as much detail as possible.

Invite learners to say what their favourite part of the story was and why.

Weekly review

Use this rubric to assess learners' progress as they worked through the activities this week.

Level	Reading	Writing	Listening and speaking
■	This group need support to sequence events in a story.	This group can use the structure of a familiar story to develop their own writing with support.	This group talk about and plan their stories well with teacher support.
●	This group can sequence events in a story.	This group are becoming more successful at using the structure of a familiar story to develop their own writing.	This group talk about and plan their stories well with minimal teacher support.
▲	This group can confidently and correctly sequence events in a story, paraphrasing as necessary without losing meaning.	This group can use the structure of a familiar story to develop their own writing.	This group plan their stories well through discussion.

End of unit assessment

Use PCM 16 to assess learners' knowledge of suffixes, prefixes, rhyming words and sentence structure. This worksheet can be used under test conditions. Either collect and mark the learners' work, or have them mark each other's work and give a score. If appropriate, record the scores.

Unit 5 Animals and us

Unit overview

This unit offers a poem, traditional story and factual information about dolphins. After some introductory work on dolphins to familiarise themselves with these animals, learners will listen to a poem about dolphins, focussing on the language used and why it was chosen.

As learners work through the unit they will read aloud, retell and talk about events and characters in a traditional story. *The Dolphin King* is a folk tale from France. They will identify and describe story characters. They will read a non-fiction passage about dolphins and learn about the layout of posters before designing their own poster.

Learners will have the opportunities to develop hearing and identifying phonemes in words, and to segment and blend phonemes to spell and read words in isolation and embedded in text.

They will have opportunities to read high frequency words and extend the range of words recognised on sight.

Reading	Writing	Listening and speaking
2R06 Read aloud with increased accuracy, fluency and expression;	2W03 Begin to reread own writing aloud to check for sense and accuracy;	2SL1 Recount experiences and explore possibilities;
2R07 Begin to read with fluency and expression, taking some notice of punctuation, including speech marks;	2W05 Use the structures of familiar poems and stories in developing own writing;	2SL3 Articulate clearly so that others can hear;
2R08 Explore a variety of non-fiction texts on screen;	2W06 Plan writing through discussion or by speaking aloud;	2SL6 Attempt to express ideas precisely, using a growing vocabulary;
2R10 Discuss the meaning of unfamiliar words encountered in reading;	2Wa4 Begin to use dialogue in stories;	2SL7 Listen carefully and respond appropriately, asking questions of others;
2Rx1 Read and respond to question words, e.g. 'what', 'where', 'when', 'who', 'why';	2Wa7 Write simple evaluations of books read;	2SL8 Demonstrate 'attentive listening' and engage with another speaker
2Rx3 Find answers to questions by reading a section of text;	2Wt1 Structure a story with a beginning, middle and end;	
2Ri2 Identify and describe story settings and characters, recognising that they may be from different times and places;	2Wp1 Write in clear sentences using capital letters, full stops and question marks;	
2Ri3 Make simple inferences from the words on the page, e.g. about feelings;	2Wp2 Find alternatives to 'and'/'then' in developing a narrative and connecting ideas;	
2Rw1 Comment on some vocabulary choices, e.g. adjectives;	2Wp3 Use mainly simple and compound sentences, with 'and'/'but' to connect ideas; 'because' may begin to be used in a complex sentence;	
2Rw2 Talk about what happens at the beginning, in the middle or at the end of a story;	2Wp4 Use past and present tenses accurately (if not always consistently);	
	2Ws1 Learn the different common spellings of long vowel phonemes;	
	2Ws2 Apply knowledge of phonemes and spelling patterns in writing independently as well as when writing sentences from memory dictated by the teacher;	

2Rv1 Show some awareness that texts have different purposes;	2Ws4 Spell words with common prefixes and suffixes, e.g. un–, dis–, –ful, –ly;	
2Rw3 Read poems and comment on words and sounds, rhyme and rhythm	2Ws3 Secure the spelling of high frequency words and common irregular words	

Related resources

- Slideshow 5: *Animals and us*
- Audio files: *Dolphin Ballet*; *The Dolphin King*; *Dolphins*
- PCM 17: Silent letters
- PCM 18: Sequencing
- PCM 19: End of unit assessment

Introducing the unit

Tell learners they are going to find out more about dolphins in this unit. Establish whether or not they have seen dolphins and whether they know much about them.

This is a good opportunity to use on-screen activities with the class. There is a wide range of information, photographs and videos about dolphins on the internet. The websites below offer information that is well suited to this age group. Select the material that you think would generate the most interest in your classroom.

- http://easyscienceforkids.com/dolphin-facts-for-kids-video/ (short film with narration detailing dolphin facts in general terms)
- http://kids.nationalgeographic.com/animals/bottlenose-dolphin/ (photos, maps, infographics and short films about different types of dolphins around the world)
- www.adoptadolphin.org.uk (short film and information sheets about dolphins in and around Wales in the UK)

Show the class images of dolphins to recap what they know about dolphins before you move onto the texts.

The work on dolphins in this unit provides a good foundation for exploring themes related to conservation, ethical treatment of animals and environmental awareness.

Week 1

Student's Book pages 41–44

Workbook page 30

Student's Book pages 41–43

Speaking and listening

1 Tell the class they are going to listen to a poem about dolphins and that they should imagine what the poet is seeing as they listen. Then ask learners to relax and close their eyes as you read the poem *Dolphin Ballet* aloud to the class.

2 The poem is called *Dolphin Ballet*. Spend some time talking about why the poet chose this title. Encourage learners to give reasons for their opinions. Let learners suggest other suitable titles for the poem.

Reading and thinking

Tell learners that they are going to read a folk tale from France. Explain that folk tales are popular stories that were passed on in spoken form, from one generation to the next, before ever being written down. In a folk tale, there

are often many versions of the same story. Discuss why this might be.

Ask learners if they know of any other folk tales, and talk about any they might have read, for example: *The Boy Who Painted Dragons* (China), *The Adventures of Pinocchio* (Italy), *The Envious Neighbour* (Japan) and *The Talkative Tortoise* (India). If they don't know any, suggest a few titles and let learners say what they might be about.

1–2 Look at the title page of *The Dolphin King* and ask learners to predict what they think the story will be about and explain why. Does the title *The Dolphin King* help them with their predictions?

3 Ask learners to read the story quietly and independently. Monitor their reading behaviours as they read, asking some learners to read aloud. Check that learners are using a range of strategies to tackle unknown words: looking at the pictures, sounding out words, using context and grammatical clues, reading on and rereading.

Draw the learners together to help with decoding of any word or words that might be causing difficulty, for example: 'knight' (page 2) and 'might' (page 2). Both words have the same rhyming pattern but 'knight' has a silent *k*.

Support: During this time, work with groups of learners who need more direct support to read the text.

After the learners have had an opportunity to read the story themselves, draw the class together and invite individuals to read while others follow the text.

Highlight and praise strategies used to decipher any new or unfamiliar words.

Spend as much time as necessary with individuals or groups to ensure accurate decoding.

Read the story to the class once they've read it themselves. They should follow the text in their books as they listen.

Spend some time ensuring the understanding of the text before moving on to the Workbook and Student's Book activities by asking questions, discussing and developing answers.

For example:

- What did Jean and his friends work at?
- What did the dolphin do when the spear stuck into it?
- Why do you think a fierce storm blew up?
- Where did the knight take Jean?

Ask learners to provide evidence from the text for their answers.

Extension: Write some words with silent letters on the whiteboard. Ask learners to read the words and to say what they notice about the words. Then ask them to underline the silent letter in each word.

Examples: 'knee', 'wrist', 'crumb', 'gnome'; 'knock', 'wrinkle', 'lamb', 'gnaw'; 'kneel', 'wrong', 'thumb', 'gnat'; 'know', 'write', 'climb', 'gnash'.

Explore the patterns of letters used after or before the silent letter. Look at the words and the position of the silent letter (the beginning or the end of the word). Use this information to establish simple statements such as:

- Silent *g* and silent *k* can be found before *n*.
- Silent *w* sometimes comes before *r* , for example, 'write'.
- Silent *b* sometimes comes before *m*, for example, 'crumb'.

Ask learners to complete PCM 17.

Workbook page 30

Reading: vocabulary
The activity highlights some vocabulary from the story. Learners are asked to draw lines from words to their meanings. Encourage learners to use a dictionary to find the words (using the initial letter) if they don't know the meaning.

Answers
hurl – to throw forcefully
spear – a long, stabbing weapon for throwing
scream – to make a loud, high cry
dive – to plunge into water
strange – unusual
whisper – to speak very softly
heal – to make healthy

Extension: More able learners can be asked to place the words in alphabetical order. They cannot do this using only initial letters, so they will need to apply some problem-solving strategies to do this.

Student's Book page 44

Reading and writing
This activity assesses understanding of the text.

Before turning to the activity, recap the concepts of 'true', 'false' and 'can't tell'. Remind the learners that they must be able to find the evidence for a true or false answer in the text.

Give some oral examples for the learners to answer 'true', 'false' and 'can't tell'.

For example:

- Jean was on the boat with his friends.
- Two of his friends were brothers,
- Jean was the oldest on the boat.
- The spear didn't hit the dolphin.

Ensure that learners know what they are being asked to do before giving them time to complete the activity.

Answers
1 fishing; a spear
2 true, can't tell, true, false, true
3 The dolphin screamed and dived beneath the waves.
4 under
5 The dolphin dived under the waves.

58

Weekly review

Use this rubric to assess learners' progress as they worked through the activities this week.

Level	Reading	Writing	Listening and speaking
■	This group read with increased accuracy but still need some support to decode unfamiliar words.	This group can write in clear sentences, using capital letters and full stops, but not always consistently.	When fully focused this group listen carefully and respond appropriately.
●	This group are beginning to read with increased accuracy, fluency and expression taking some notice of punctuation.	This group can write in clear sentences, using capital letters and full stops and are beginning to write with a variety of sentence types.	This group mostly listen carefully and respond appropriately.
▲	This group read with increased accuracy, fluency and expression, taking some notice of punctuation including speech marks.	This group can write in clear sentences, using capital letters and full stops. They write with a variety of sentence types.	This group demonstrate attentive listening and engage with another speaker. They listen carefully and respond appropriately.

Week 2

Student's Book pages 45–47

Workbook pages 31–33

Workbook page 31

Sounds and spelling

Revise the concept of two letters representing one sound as necessary. Invite the learners to give examples: *sh, ch, oo, ai, oa*.

Ask learners to give examples of words with the sound *sh* at the beginning/at the end, and then ask them to write a few of the suggested words on mini-whiteboards. Keep this activity short and quick before moving on to the two letters *ph* representing one sound.

Write these words on the whiteboard: 'dolphin', 'photograph', 'elephant', 'graph', 'alphabet', 'telephone'.

Ask learners to look at the words and say what they all have in common (*ph*). Ask learners if they can read any or all of the words. Invite them to read a chosen word and say what sound the two letters *ph* represent (the same sound as the alphabet letter *f*).

Ask learners to underline the letters *ph* in each word. The *ph* words above are the ones that learners at this stage are most likely to use.

The learners should then complete Workbook page 31.

Extension: Investigate some other sounds with some groups of learners. For example:

- *ch* representing *sh*, as in' chef', 'chiffon', 'chute', 'machine' and 'parachute'
- *ch* representing *k*, as in 'chemist', 'character', 'Michael', 'Christmas'.

Answers
dolphin, photograph, telephone, alphabet, elephant, graph

Workbook page 32

Sounds and spelling

Write the following words on the board and ask learners to look at the similarities and differences in each pair of words.

'hand' – 'handful'

'care' – 'careful'

'help' – 'helpful'

'forget' – 'forgetful'

'use' – 'useful'

'pain' – 'painful'

Invite learners to highlight the part of each word that makes it different from its partner (–*ful*).

Tell the learners that –*ful* is a suffix and that a suffix is a group of letters added to the end of a word to make a new word. It is important that

59

the learners know and remember that only one *l* is needed when –*ful* is a suffix.

Dictation

Give the learners some practice in writing words with the suffix –*ful*. Using mini-whiteboards and pens, ask learners to write words that you dictate.

Sentences with a controlled vocabulary are good for spelling practice and you could include one dictated sentence at the end of a number of dictated words. This allows previously taught phonemes and high frequency words to be revisited regularly.

Examples for dictation:

- He was careful lifting the jam tarts.
- She has a painful cut on her arm.
- A spade is a useful garden tool.

Take opportunities to highlight words with the suffix –*ful* in text during the learning period.

The learners should then turn to page 32 which includes:

1 adding a suffix to words and writing the new word

2 completing sentences from a choice of root word/root word + suffix

3 choosing two words to use in sentences.

Extension: Work in groups with the learners to investigate another common suffix –*less*.

Examples:

'care' + *less*

'hope' + *less*

'use' + *less*

'pain' + *less*

'help' + *less*

Answers
1 helpful, painful, handful, careful, useful, hopeful, playful
2 care, careful
3 Learners' own answers.

Student's Book page 45

Reading and writing

This section focuses on vocabulary: the meanings of words, using vocabulary correctly and making simple inferences from the words on the page.

1 Learners choose words to complete sentences. Check that learners can read the

words out of context, and that they know the meanings of the words.

Support: Work with individuals or a small group, helping with decoding, modelling reading and discussing the choice of word for each sentence. This allows you to assess the learners understanding of the meanings of the words without allowing any difficulties with decoding to get in the way.

2 Learners choose words from the text that imply that actions started/were carried out in a certain way.

3–5 These questions focus on different words ('shout', 'whisper') to describe the ways people can speak.

Ask learners to scan the story to find out how the knight was feeling when he spoke to the fishermen. What word lets them know that?

Similarly, ask learners to say why they think the knight 'whispered' to Jean. Discuss with the learners why the author may have chosen that word when he could have used the word 'said'.

Before learners turn to the questions, remind them what to include in their sentences: capital letters, full stops, interesting vocabulary, accurate spelling, joining of letters in handwriting. Decide how many criteria to focus on for individuals and groups of learners.

Remind the learners to reread their work aloud and to check if their sentences include the points asked for.

Answers
1 hurled, fierce, strange, whispered, removed
2 suddenly, gently
3–5 Learners' own answers.

Student's Book page 46

Reading and writing

1 Assess the learners' understanding of the story by asking them: Who said it? Jean, the dolphin king or the knight?

2 Ask learners to write the next part of the story, that is what happens after Jean promises never to hunt dolphins again.

3 Before turning to question 3, discuss with the learners words that would describe Jean at the beginning of the story and words that would describe Jean at the end of the story, eliciting words that appear in the box. Had Jean changed? Why do the learners think he changed?

Ask learners to read the words in the box. Are any of the words that they suggested in the box? What do they notice about some of the words? Make sure they can see that some have suffixes.

Answers
1 Jean/the knight/Jean/the knight/the dolphin king/Jean
2 Learners' own answers.
3 brave, honest, fearless, truthful

Listening and talking
Learners work in pairs to answer the questions.

Answers
1–2 Learners' own answers.

Workbook page 33
Reading
Before learners turn to this activity, ask them to reread the story. Discuss strategies for putting the sentences in order.

- Read all the sentences first before writing any numbers.
- Look for possible clues – is there a sentence that is obviously first? Think back to the story. What happened first? Similarly, is there a sentence that is obviously last?
- What had to happen to make something else happen? For example: Jean hurled his spear at a dolphin and then the dolphin screamed and dived beneath the waves.
- Look for words like 'then' and 'next'. These words mean that something else had to have happened before that part of the story.
- Read and reread. Is the order making sense? Check with the text if necessary.

Support: Support learners by giving them PCM 18. This will allow them to out the sentences and physically rearrange them till they get the most satisfactory order.

Student's Book page 47
Sounds and spelling
Before turning to the spelling patterns *ai + r = air* (as in 'hair') and *ea + r = ear* (as in 'dear'), revise the spelling patterns *ar*, *or* and *er* by:

- asking learners to generate words with each of the spelling patterns
- asking learners to write words with each of the spelling patterns.

1–4 Write a selection of words that end with *–air* and *–ear* on the whiteboard, for example: 'hair', 'dear', 'year', 'chair', 'pair', 'near'. Ask learners to sort the words for each spelling pattern and then to generate more words for each.

For example: 'hair', 'chair', 'pair', 'fair', 'stair'; 'dear', 'year', 'near', 'fear', 'clear', 'hear', 'gear'.

Ensure that learners know the meanings of the words particularly words like 'hair', 'pair', 'fair', 'stair' and 'hear' which have homophones.

5 Before the learners turn to question 5, write the words 'far'/'fair', 'star'/'stair' on the whiteboard. Discuss with them what they notice about the pairs of words and how one letter changes the way we read the word and what it means.

Dictation
Some or all of these sentences can be used for dictation and spelling.

- Jack sat on a high chair.
- He has a new pair of boots.
- Max has short hair.
- She sits near to me in the class.
- I can hear the sound of bells.

Extension: Investigate with the learners other representations of *–air* and *–ear*, such as *–are* making homophones of *–air* words, and *–ere* making homophones of *–ear* words.

Examples: 'hare'/'hair'; 'here'/'hear'; 'stare'/'stair'; 'pear'/'pair'; 'fare'/'fair'.

Ask learners to make pairs of illustrated cards to show the differences in meaning.

Answers
1 fear, dear, hear, near, clear, spear, shear
2 clear, near, hear
3 chair, fair, hair, stair, pair
4 pair, hair, chair
5 Learners' own sentences.

Weekly review

Use this rubric to assess learners' progress as they worked through the activities this week.

Level	Reading	Writing
■	This group are making progress developing their understanding of vocabulary and text through discussion and when answering questions.	This group are making good progress at applying knowledge of phonemes and spelling patterns when writing sentences dictated by the teacher.
●	This group show understanding of vocabulary and text through discussion and when answering questions.	This group apply knowledge of phonemes and spelling patterns when writing sentences dictated by the teacher. They usually apply this knowledge when writing independently.
▲	This group show a thorough understanding of vocabulary and text through discussion and when answering questions.	This group apply knowledge of phonemes and spelling patterns in writing independently as well as when writing sentences dictated by the teacher.

Week 3

Student's Book pages 48–50

Workbook pages 34–35

Student's Book page 48

Reading and writing

This section focuses on vocabulary to describe weather, discussing the vocabulary and when it might be used. Learners use some of the vocabulary to describe a scene.

1 Learners choose and write words that could describe a fierce storm.

2 Learners imagine a situation when they are outside when a storm starts.

Tell learners that the writing needs to focus on:

- where they were when the storm happened
- what they did during the storm, and where they sheltered
- what they did after the storm.

Tell learners they should use some of the vocabulary in activity 1 when they describe the storm.

Discuss with the learners what they need to include in their stories and set targets. Give them time to work in pairs to talk and develop ideas for their story.

Support: Support some individuals by scribing their story as they tell it. This allows learners who may have difficulty with handwriting,

organisational skills, and/or spelling to create and tell their story.

After writing, invite some learners to read their stories to the class and ask their peers to say what they liked about the story.

Use the reading of the stories to highlight any teaching points needing to be addressed.

3 Ask learners to write, in order, words that describe different strengths of wind.

Answers
1 heavy rain, high waves, strong winds, dark clouds, downpours, thunder and lightning
2 Learners' own answers.
3 breeze, gale, hurricane

Student's Book page 49

Reading and writing

Before turning to the activity, ask learners to think of the whole story *The Dolphin King* and divide it into three parts.

1 Ask learners to say what the three main parts of the story are – the beginning – before the storm, the middle – during the storm, and the end – after the storm.

Discuss with the learners which part of the story:

- sets the scene
- tells about what happens
- finishes the story.

2–4 These questions focus on the meaning of a 'promise' and give learners the opportunity to talk about promises that they have made.

Workbook page 34

Reading and writing

Use these questions to assess how well learners understand alphabetical order. Allow them to check and correct each other's work. They can do the word search individually or in pairs.

Answers
1 boat, dolphin, friend, storm; knight, spear, waves.
2

w	b	x	s	u	z	k
d	o	l	p	h	i	n
w	a	v	e	s	y	i
c	t	j	a	q	u	g
s	t	o	r	m	v	h
f	r	i	e	n	d	t

Workbook page 35

Writing

Learners are given another opportunity to write a book review, this time about a different type of story from that of *Kind Emma*. It gives them the opportunity to express likes and dislikes in stories.

After writing, take the opportunity to discuss which story the learners liked best and why. Talk about:

- what Jean did that was wrong

- why learners think Jean said he could throw a spear better than his friends could

- whether learners think Jean had thought about the consequences of his actions

- what actions Jean had done that were good.

Extension: To round off the study of *The Dolphin King*, organise the learners to design and make a collage for a class display of the world in which the dolphin king lives.

Student's Book page 50

Reading

Before learners read the passage about dolphins on page 50, discuss what they already know about dolphins from the introduction and what they've read. Try to elicit some of the vocabulary and information that they will meet in the passage. This prepares the learners for meeting words and concepts that might be unfamiliar in the text.

Read the passage *Dolphins* with the learners, helping with decoding and modelling reading.

Discuss what type of text it is, comparing it with *The Dolphin King*.

Listening and speaking

Give learners time to work in pairs to discuss:

- the different ways that humans can cause dolphins to die

- how oil can injure and cause dolphins to die.

Writing

Discuss conservation with the class and what some people do to protect animals.

Learners then design a poster about an event to raise money for a Dolphin Conservation Charity.

Discuss with learners what they need to think about to make their poster attractive and make people want to read it. What information needs to be on the poster and how it should be written? If possible, spend some time looking at examples of posters on screen. The websites used earlier in this unit have examples that can be used as a starting point.

Weekly review

Use this rubric to assess learners' progress as they worked through the activities this week.

Level	Reading	Writing
■	This group needs support to use strategies when the text is unfamiliar.	With teacher support this group can structure a story with a beginning, a middle and an end.
●	This group are making very good progress with using a variety of strategies to read a piece of unfamiliar text.	This group can structure a story with a beginning, a middle and an end and are beginning to use interesting words.
▲	This group can use a variety of strategies to read a piece of unfamiliar text, switching naturally to the most helpful strategy.	This group can structure a story with a beginning, a middle and an end and use interesting words and phrases.

End of unit assessment

Use PCM 19 to review the work done in this unit. Hand out the sheets and ask learners work under test conditions to complete the sheet independently. Collect the sheets and mark them or allow learners to mark each other's sheets by displaying a prepared answer key. Record the results, taking note of which learners may need more practice or support.

Unit 6 Staying Safe

Unit overview

As learners work through this unit, they will read aloud with increased fluency and accuracy while they explore a non-fiction text. *World's Deadliest Creatures* is an information book about dangerous creatures. Learners will read factual information from text, maps, photographs and charts. They will learn about reading charts for information before adding information to a chart.

The unit could be part of a study about staying safe in the wider sense.

Learners will have the opportunity to identify syllables and to use the breaking of words into syllables as a spelling strategy.

They will have opportunities to read high frequency words and other familiar words.

Reading	Writing	Listening and speaking
2R06 Read aloud with increased accuracy, fluency and expression; 2R03 Identify syllables and split familiar compound words into parts; 2R04 Extend the range of common words recognised on sight; 2R05 Begin to develop likes and dislikes in reading and listening to stories drawing on background information and vocabulary provided; 2R07 Begin to read with fluency and expression, taking some notice of punctuation, including speech marks; 2R10 Discuss the meaning of unfamiliar words encountered in reading; 2Rx1 Read and respond to question words, e.g. 'what', 'where', 'when', 'who', 'why'; 2Rx3 Find answers to questions by reading a section of text; 2Rx4 Find factual information from different formats, e.g. charts, labelled diagrams; 2Rv1 Show some awareness that texts have different purposes; 2Rv2 Identify general features of known text types	2W03 Begin to reread own writing aloud to check for sense and accuracy; 2Wa7 Write simple evaluations of books read; 2Wa3 Build and use collections of interesting and significant words; 2Wa5 Use features of chosen text type; 2Wp1 Write in clear sentences using capital letters, full stops and question marks; 2Wp3 Use mainly simple and compound sentences, with 'and'/'but' to connect ideas; 'because' may begin to be used in a complex sentence; 2Ws1 Learn the different common spellings of long vowel phonemes; 2Ws2 Apply knowledge of phonemes and spelling patterns in writing independently as well as when writing sentences from memory dictated by the teacher; 2Ws3 Secure the spelling of high frequency words and common irregular words	2SL1 Recount experiences and explore possibilities; 2SL3 Articulate clearly so that others can hear; 2SL6 Attempt to express ideas precisely, using a growing vocabulary; 2SL7 Listen carefully and respond appropriately, asking questions of others; 2SL8 Demonstrate 'attentive listening' and engage with another speaker

Related resources

- Slideshow 6: Staying safe
- Audio file: *World's Deadliest Creatures*
- PCM 20: Syllables
- PCM 21: Phonics *ow*
- PCM 22: End of unit assessment

Introducing the unit

Discuss with the learners how they keep themselves safe. Tell them that there are things that all children need to do to keep themselves safe no matter where they live, such as keeping out of dangerous buildings, staying away from boiling water, always letting their parents know where they are going. Allow learners to suggest more ways of remaining safe and list these for the classroom.

Explain that one of the ways in which we can stay safe is to be aware of dangers around us.

Some of these dangers are in the form of plants that are poisonous or animals that are dangerous. Discuss which plants and animals are dangerous in your area.

Tell the class that they are going to learn more about some animals that are very dangerous. Stress that these animals are only dangerous under certain conditions, normally when they are threatened, and that for the most part, they don't harm people at all.

Week 1

Student's Book pages 51–55

Workbook pages 36–37

Display the image of the front cover of *World's Deadliest Creatures*.

Read the title together and look at the photograph. Ask the learners how they feel. What do they think when they see the spider? What makes the learners think that the creature could be deadly? What would the creature do to make it deadly?

Ask the learners if they or anyone in their family have ever seen a deadly creature.

Student's Book page 51

Reading and writing

Before learners turn to the activity, ask them to look at the contents page of *World's Deadliest Creatures* and say what a contents page is and what it is used for.

Ask learners what they will find out about on page 4. When an answer is given ask learners to turn to page 4 to check that the heading matches page 4 of the contents page. Repeat this for other pages.

Learners should then answer the questions before moving onto a guided reading of the material.

Answer
1 animals that are dangerous
2 World's Deadliest Creatures
3 non-fiction or information book
4 Anna Claybourne
5 The book is not illustrated. It contains photographs.
6 nasty stings
7 deadliest poison
8 page 12

Student's Book pages 52–54

Reading

Give learners time to look at the photographs on pages 1–2 of the text before inviting them to tell any information that they have got from the photographs.

Move on to ask questions such as:

- Which creatures are dangerous? How do you know they are dangerous?

- Which is the largest creature? How does the photograph suggest that the whale shark is not dangerous?

- Are you always able to tell just by looking at a creature if it is dangerous?

Invite a learner to read the header of the chapter ('Deadly or not?' and discuss what a 'heading' is.

Read pages 1–2 together before inviting individuals to read aloud.

Discuss the contents of the pages and how the header says what the reader will read about.

Direct the learners' attention to pages 3–4 and invite a learner to say what the header is. Read the pages together and ask the learners to say what information they found out by reading. Talk about 'venom'/'venomous' and 'fangs' ensuring that the learners understand the meanings of the words.

Next, direct the learners' attention to the maps, asking what information they can get from them. Discuss the places where the deadly creatures are found and ensure that learners understand what the symbols mean.

Ask learners to work in pairs and to choose a page to read together. Tell them that they need to find one piece of information to tell their classmates. Monitor and support learners where necessary.

Invite pairs of learners to say what information they found out.

Discuss with the learners that it is not necessary to read this type of book from the first page to the last. Why not?

Ask learners to read to the end of the book. Praise them for using strategies to work out any unknown words.

Support: Work with individuals or groups who need support to apply strategies to read the text.

Read through the book with the learners, stopping to discuss meanings of words and to ask questions on each chapter, such as:

- Where would you find deathstalker scorpions?
- How does the blue-ringed octopus attack?
- What is the most poisonous creature in the world?

Workbook page 36

Reading

Learners are asked to match the creatures to their names.

Answer

whale shark, spitting cobra, box jellyfish, golden poison dart frog, funnel-web spider, scorpion

Student's Book page 55

Reading and writing

Before learners turn to the activity, ask them what parts of a non-fiction book can give information, for example: photographs, captions, labels, diagrams, pictures, charts, maps and text. To answer the questions on page 55, learners will need to read text, look at photographs and look at maps.

Draw learners' attention to the layout of the questions and invite them to tell you what they notice. The page numbers are given for reference.

- Ask learners to read the question that they will find the answers to on, say, page 3.
- Ask the learners to choose any question, to read it and say what page they will find the answer on.

Read through all the questions with the learners before the learners complete the activity.

Answer

page 1 golden poison dart frog; whale shark; the frog has the word 'dangerous!' next to it and the shark doesn't
page 2 blue-ringed octopus
page 3 it bites with venomous fangs; Australia
page 4 it can spit venom at your eyes; African countries, India, China
page 5 it can sting you with its tail; North African countries, Middle Eastern countries
page 6 a large number of bees together; over 20,000; USA, Central American countries, South American countries, African countries

Workbook page 37

Reading

In this activity learners match words that they have read in the text to their meanings. Remind learners to read all the words and meanings before matching.

Support: Work with individuals, or a small group, who may need help with decoding. This will allow you to assess their understanding of vocabulary without the decoding getting in the way.

Answer

venom – harmful chemical injected when an animal bites you
poisonous – dangerous to eat or touch
swarm – a big group of insects
tentacles – long, dangly body parts used for feeding or moving about
fangs – sharp teeth which inject poison
creature – an animal, especially a non-human
dangerous – unsafe

v

Weekly review

Use this rubric to assess learners' progress as they worked through the activities this week.

Level	Reading	Writing	Listening and speaking
■	These learners can find information from pictures and maps but need some support to find information from continuous text.	These learners can write the answers to questions writing the information needed.	These learners attempt to express ideas clearly. They are using a growing vocabulary in topics of interest.
●	With minimal support these learners can find factual information from different formats.	These learners can answer questions in clear sentences but sometimes need reminding to use capital letters and full stops.	These learners attempt to express ideas clearly using a growing vocabulary.
▲	These learners can find factual information from different formats.	These learners can answer questions in clear sentences, using capital letters and full stops.	These learners attempt to express ideas clearly using a growing vocabulary. They are able to extend their ideas in the light of discussion.

Week 2

Student's Book pages 56–58

Workbook pages 38–39

Student's Book page 56

Reading and writing

1 Learners should read the information pages 52–54 again, by themselves or in pairs. Give them some time to talk about the content before they complete activity 2.

2 Learners copy and complete the sentences.

Answers
2 blue-ringed octopus; tiger shark; box jellyfish

Speaking and listening

Ask learners to work in pairs, or groups of about three, to discuss why people need water. Tell them that they will be asked to tell some information to their peers, after they have discussed it with their partner.

Writing

1–2 Learners should complete these written activities after reporting to their peers about why people need water.

Workbook page 39

Sounds and spelling

This activity focuses on discriminating syllables firstly in spoken words and then discriminating and identifying them in written words. Each beat in a word is a syllable:

teach   /   er
↓   ↓
syllable 1   syllable 2

Say a name and then clap the syllables as you say the name slowly, emphasising the syllables, for example: Shak/il/a, Ah/med, Kate, So/phie, Ma/til/da, Na/rin/der, Ad/am, Zain, Dai/sy.

Ask learners to say their name and clap the syllables.

Explain that a syllable is a beat, so 'Kate' has one beat, 'So/phie' has two beats and 'Ma/til/da' has three beats.

It is important that the learners understand the concept of syllables in words and use it as a strategy for spelling.

The following rhyme is useful for reminding learners to break words up for spelling. Teach the rhyme to the learners and come back to it on other occasions.

Can't spell a word? Don't be absurd!

Be proud, say the word out loud

elephant

Don't frown, just break it down

el – e – phant

Be smart, stretch out each part

e – l – e – ph – a – n – t

Take a look, take a real good look.

1–2 Turn to the words needed in Question 1: 'lizard', 'spider', 'octopus', 'cobra', 'scorpion', 'frog'. Ask learners to say and clap the number of syllables in each word.

Demonstrate using the rhyme to spell one of the words before asking learners to spell the others, for example: scorpion: scor/pi/on; s – c – o – r – p – i – o – n

The learners should now turn to Activities 1 and 2.

3–4 Learners are asked to write the two small words that make up the word 'jellyfish', and to make compound words using 'fish' as one of the small words.

Answers
1 liz/ard (2), spi/der (2), oct/o/pus (3), co/bra (2), scor/pi/on (3), frog (1)
2 an/i/mal, spi/der, ven/om
3 jelly, fish
4 goldfish, starfish, swordfish

Student's Book page 57

Reading and writing

This activity introduces learners to finding information from a chart.

Ask learners to look at page 57, and demonstrate to them how to read a chart like this:

- Point to the words on the left-hand side and run your finger down the words.
- Ask learners to do the same on their books.
- Point to the words at the top and run your finger across the words.
- Ask the learners to read the words in the left-hand column.
- Ask the learners to read the words along the top of the chart.

- Demonstrate how to find information from the chart for example:
    1 Does a bee bite, spit or sting?
    Show learners how to find the word 'bee' and then run their finger along until they come to a tick. Look to the top to find the answer – 'sting'.
    2 Which creatures sting their prey?
    Show learners how this time they need to find the word 'sting' at the top of the chart and run their finger down until they come to a tick and then take their finger back to the left until they find the name of the creature.

Note: The learners need to find more than one creature that stings.

Support: Some learners may require support with this task. They may find it difficult to hold the information in their heads and coordinate the skills required to find information from the chart.

1 Learners read the chart to answer the questions.

2 Learners are asked to write a list of animals that are not safe to touch. For this activity, ask them to think about animals that they have not been learning about in this unit.

3 The learners write a list of animals that are safe to touch.

Answers
1 spits; spider, octopus, shark; scorpion, bee
2 Learners' own answers.
3 Learners' own answers.

Workbook page 38

Reading and writing

Before learners turn to the activity, demonstrate how to fill in Workbook page 38 – where to put ticks in boxes.

In this activity, learners look down the column at the left-hand side, read the name of the creature and the page where they will find the information, for example: 'spider', 'page 3'. The learners look at page 3, look at the map to find the name of the country and then return to the Workbook, put their finger on the word 'spider' and run it along until they come to the name of the country at the top (Australia), and then they put a tick in the box.

Repeat the process for the other creatures.

2 Learners read the completed chart to find information.

Support: Support learners that need help reading the chart. They may have difficulty putting 'ticks' in the correct box, not because they can't read the words but because, for example, of an organisational difficulty.

Extension: Ask learners to research another deadly animal that they haven't been reading about, using text or the internet. They should then write about the animal in the style of *World's Deadliest Creatures* and illustrate their writing. This could be a school task or a task to be done at home and brought into school.

A new 'book' could be made about the world's deadliest creatures.

Student's Book page 58

Sounds and spelling

This activity gives learners further practice in identifying syllables and completing words where a syllable is missing.

The first activity uses the names of creatures in the text while the second activity asks the learners to identify syllables in the names of the months of the year.

Before learners turn to the activity, give some oral practice in identifying syllables in words, for example, the days of the week could be used: Mon/day, Tues/day, Wed/nes/day, Thurs/day, Fri/day, Sat/ur/day, Sun/day.

Draw the learners' attention to 'Monday'. It sounds like 'Munday' but is written 'Monday'.

Write some words on the whiteboard with a syllable missing, for example: cro/__/dile, ba/__/na, el/__/phant, for/__/ful, com/__/ter, din/_ /saur.

1 Learners are asked to add missing syllables to words in sentences and then to copy the sentences correctly.

2 Learners are asked to add the missing syllable to the name of each month of the year and then to write the names of the months correctly.

Encourage learners to learn rhymes associated with the months of the year, for example:

30 days hath September,

April, June and November.

All the rest have 31

Except for February alone,

Which has but 28 days clear

And 29 in each leap year.

Answers

1 spi/er, cob/ra, scor/pi/on, oc/to/pus, jel/ly/fish
2 Jan/u/ar/y, Feb/ru/ar/y, March, Ap/ril, May, June, Jul/y, Au/gust, Sep/tem/ber, Oc/to/ber, No/vem/ber, De/cem/ber

Extension: Ask learners to find out about 'parts of the day' words, for example: 'dawn', 'sunrise', 'morning', 'midday', 'noon', 'afternoon', 'dusk', 'twilight', 'sunset', 'evening', 'night', 'midnight'.

Use PCM 20 to reinforce and consolidate work on syllables. Activity A gives learners further practise in identifying syllables, and Activity B asks learners to write words using syllables that are in the wrong order.

Weekly review

Use this rubric to assess learners' progress as they worked through the activities this week.

Level	Reading	Writing	Listening and speaking
■	This group can find information from charts with teacher support. They are developing an understanding of the concept of syllables in words.	With teacher support this group can use information to complete a chart.	At times this group need teacher support to focus and respond appropriately.
●	This group can find factual information from charts. They understand the concept of syllables and use it as a strategy for reading.	This group can use information to complete a chart with minimal support.	This group listen carefully and respond appropriately most of the time.
▲	This group can confidently find factual information from charts. They understand the concept of syllables and are beginning to use it as a strategy for reading.	This group can use information to complete a chart.	This group listen carefully and respond appropriately at all times.

Week 3

Student's Book pages 59–60

Workbook pages 40–41

Workbook page 40

Reading

Before turning to the activity, discuss with the learners what a 'habitat' is.

Learners should know that a habitat is a place where an animal lives. It provides the animal with food, water and shelter. There are many different habitats around the world that animals live in.

Widen the discussion from the creatures that they have been reading about to other types of animals.

Identify different habitats, for example: desert, forest, mountains, ocean, jungle, ice and snow, underground.

Write the names of habitats as headings on the whiteboard. If necessary, limit the headings to the ones that appear on Workbook page 40: ocean, jungle, ice and snow, underground.

Say the names of animals and ask learners which habitat they would be found in. Ask a learner to write the name under the correct heading.

Give learners the opportunity of suggesting names of animals to write under the correct heading.

Turn to Workbook page 40 and ask learners to look at the pictures and read the names of the animals. Ask them to identify any picture or name of an animal that they are unsure of. Take time to discuss the animals and read the names before the learners complete the activity.

Student's Book page 59

Sounds and spelling

This section focuses on how the same spelling pattern can represent different sounds, and that additional text is sometimes required to determine pronunciation.

For example: I will read the book tonight.

I read the book last night.

Write words on the whiteboard with the letter string *ea* representing different sounds.

Suggested words: 'head', 'seat', 'bear', 'thread', 'pear', 'bread', 'leaf', 'wear', 'neat', 'meat'.

Ask learners to group the words according to the sound that *ea* represents. They write the words in three lists on mini-whiteboards. Discuss why the learners have grouped the words in the way that they have.

Write 'tear', 'read' and 'lead' on the whiteboard and ask learners to read them. Explain that additional text is required to determine the pronunciation of the words.

Invite learners to say sentences that show the different pronunciations and meanings of the words.

Answers
1 sounds like 'peach': beach, teach, reach; sounds like 'bread': head, thread; sounds like 'pear': bear, tear, wear

Listening and speaking

Learners read the sentences and talk about the underlined words with a partner.

Sounds and spelling

Learners complete the rhymes using words from the box.

Answers
1 Lead rhymes with head.
2 Read rhymes with bead.

Dictation

Use these or similar sentences for spelling related dictation in this unit.

- The fish swam in the sea.
- I banged my head on the chair.
- This pear is very ripe.
- The bread is stale.

The letters *ow* can also represent different sounds in words. At a later date, use the following words to teach this: 'snow', 'grow', 'cow', 'town', 'flow', 'brown', 'show', 'owl', 'flower', 'now', 'towel'.

Use the words 'bow', 'sow', 'row' to show that additional text is required to determine the pronunciation of the words.

Use PCM 21 to consolidate and assess the *ow* sound.

Student's Book page 60

Speaking and listening

This activity brings learners back to the beginning of the unit by focusing on dangers that all children should be aware of.

1 Learners work in pairs, look at the pictures and discuss the potential dangers.

Draw the learners together and discuss the picture, inviting individual learners to comment on the pictures.

2 Learners are asked to write sentences that tell of the dangers in each picture.

Workbook page 41

Writing

The learners are given another opportunity to write a book review. This time they review a non-fiction book. After writing, take the opportunity to discuss which type of book the learners liked best and why.

Weekly review

Use this rubric to assess learners' progress as they worked through the activities this week.

Level	Reading	Writing	Listening and speaking
■	This group are beginning to use context along with phonics to read words where the pronunciation is determined by meaning.	This group can write sentences, most of the time remembering capital letters and full stops. They are beginning to introduce interesting words to their sentences.	This group enjoy talking in pairs. They sometimes need support to keep to the topic under discussion and to take turns to listen and to speak.
●	This group understand the concept of letter strings representing different sounds and can use context to read the word.	This group can write in clear sentences and are beginning to use more interesting words and phrases of description.	This group work well when talking in pairs. They usually 'stick' to the topic under discussion, taking turns to listen and to speak.
▲	This group fully understand the concept of letter strings representing different sounds and can use context to read the word.	This group can write in clear sentences using interesting words and phrases of description.	This group work well when talking in pairs. They 'stick' to the topic under discussion, taking turns to listen and to speak.

End of unit assessment

Use PCM 22 to consolidate and assess the work done on charts in this unit. Check that learners are able to classify animals by habitat correctly and that they complete the chart correctly. Their answers to the questions should indicate that they are able to read the chart.

Unit 7 When Arthur Wouldn't Sleep

Unit overview

In this unit, learners will deal with the ideas of sleep and dreaming as they read a fantasy story called *When Arthur Wouldn't Sleep* as well as *The Moon-Baby*, a traditional lullaby from Africa.

As learners work through this unit they will develop their reading skills, reading with increased accuracy, fluency and expression, taking some notice of punctuation including speech. They will have the opportunity to talk about what is happening in the story and to develop their understanding of meaning in text.

They will have the opportunity to develop their writing skills taking account of punctuation and increased use of accurate spelling.

Reading	Writing	Listening and speaking
2R06 Read aloud with increased accuracy, fluency and expression; 2R07 Begin to read with fluency and expression, taking some notice of punctuation, including speech marks; 2R10 Discuss the meaning of unfamiliar words encountered in reading; 2Rx1 Read and respond to question words, e.g. 'what', 'where', 'when', 'who', 'why'; 2Rx3 Find answers to questions by reading a section of text; 2Ri2 Identify and describe story settings and characters, recognising that they may be from different times and places; 2Ri3 Make simple inferences from the words on the page, e.g. about feelings; 2Rw1 Comment on some vocabulary choices, e.g. adjectives; 2R03 Identify syllables and split familiar compound words into parts; 2R04 Extend the range of common words recognised on sight	2W03 Begin to reread own writing aloud to check for sense and accuracy; 2W06 Plan writing through discussion or by speaking aloud; 2Wa1 Develop stories with a setting, characters and a sequence of events; 2Wa5 Use features of chosen text type; 2Wp1 Write in clear sentences using capital letters, full stops and question marks; 2Wp3 Use mainly simple and compound sentences, with 'and'/'but' to connect ideas; 'because may begin to be used in a complex sentence; 2Wp4 Use past and present tenses accurately (if not always consistently); 2Wp5 Begin to vary sentence openings, e.g. with simple adverbs; 2Wp6 Write with a variety of sentence types; 2Ws1 Learn the different common spellings of long vowel phonemes; 2Ws2 Apply knowledge of phonemes and spelling patterns in writing independently as well as when writing sentences from memory dictated by the teacher; 2Ws3 Secure the spelling of high frequency words and common irregular words; 2Ws4 Spell words with common prefixes and suffixes, e.g. *un–*, *dis–*, *–ful*, *–ly*	2SL1 Recount experiences and explore possibilities; 2SL3 Articulate clearly so that others can hear; 2SL6 Attempt to express ideas precisely, using a growing vocabulary; 2SL7 Listen carefully and respond appropriately, asking questions of others; 2SL8 Demonstrate 'attentive listening' and engage with another speaker; 2SL9 Extend experiences and ideas through roleplay

Related resources

- Slideshow 7: *When Arthur Wouldn't Sleep*
- Audio files: *When Arthur Wouldn't Sleep*; *The Moon-Baby*
- PCM 23: Common suffixes
- PCM 24: Words with soft *c*
- PCM 25: End of unit assessment

Introducing the unit

The character in the story (Arthur) imagines that he can see animal shapes in the clouds. If possible, take the learners outside to look at real clouds. Ask them if they can find any shapes or objects in the cloud patterns.

In the classroom, show images of cloud shapes. Ask learners to say what animals they can find in the clouds.

Ask learners to imagine they are a cloud animal. Let them tell each other which animal they are and to describe what they can see and do as they float across the sky.

Week 1

Student's Book pages 61–65

Workbook page 42

Students' Book pages 61–63

Reading and listening

Introduce the story to the learners by showing the cover of *When Arthur Wouldn't Sleep*.

Discuss the cover asking questions such as:

- What is the title of the book?
- Which character do you think Arthur is?
- Why do you think he didn't want to sleep?
- What do you think Arthur might do?
- What do you think the story is going to be about?

Ask the learners to share their own experiences of not being able or willing to go to sleep – not tired, too excited, thinking they are missing something, something on their mind – perhaps a worry or something that is going to happen.

Discuss how the learners feel when that happens and then how they feel next morning when they haven't had a good sleep. How do the learners think Arthur was feeling?

Read page 1 to the class, the write 'bedtime', 'butterflies', 'grasshoppers' and 'bees' on the whiteboard.

Try to 'slow speak' the words as you write them, to draw attention to the compound words, the syllables and the sounds that make up the words. It is good practice to model how to use strategies for reading and spelling.

Ask learners to find the words 'bedtime', 'butterflies', 'grasshoppers' and 'bees' on page 1,

before asking them to read the page quietly and independently.

After reading, ask the learners to find a word on the page that would suggest that Arthur wasn't feeling very happy ('grumbled').

Walk the learners through the story, looking at the pictures and discussing what is happening. At this point, identify any words that the learners might find tricky, such as 'competition', 'amazing', 'Crazylegs'. Write them on the whiteboard and support the learners to use strategies to read the words.

Example: 'competition'

Can learners break the word into syllables com/pe/ti/tion? They should be able to sound out the first three syllables – com/pe/ti – and that should give them the lead into –tion and so finish reading the word.

Ask learners to read the story quietly and independently. Monitor, asking individual readers to read short pieces of text aloud. Check that learners are using a range of strategies to tackle unknown words.

Support: During this time, work with a group of learners who need more direct help to apply the strategies.

Draw the class together and invite individuals to read while others follow the text. Highlight and praise strategies used to decipher any new or unfamiliar words.

Spend time ensuring the understanding of the text before moving on to Workbook and Student's Book activities by asking questions, discussing and developing answers. For example:

- Who took Arthur to meet the ladybird?
- Who won the competition?

- Read page 2 again. What was really happening to Arthur?
- What word tells the reader that Flora was tired and didn't really want to talk? (page 1)
- Why do you think it was called a Crazylegs Dancing Competition?

Workbook page 42

Writing

The activity asks learners to label the pictures of the characters with their names. The names are written in the box.

After the activity, invite learners to say how they knew which word to choose. For example:

- I was looking for a word that starts with a capital *A* for 'Arthur'.
- I was looking for a word that starts with a capital *F* for 'Flora'.
- I read 'bee'. It starts with a *b* and has two letters making one sound –*ee*.
- I read 'sheep'. It starts with *sh* and it has double *ee*.

Modelling strategies reinforces how they work.

Answers

Arthur, Flora, bee, butterfly, sheep, ladybird, hippo, grasshopper

Student's Book page 64

Reading and writing

1–2 Before turning to the questions, discuss the meaning of 'main character'. Who is the main character in this story? Why is he called the main character?

Ask learners to think of other stories that have a main character. Who is the main character in *Jodie the Juggler*? Who is the main character in *Kind Emma*? Who is the main character in *The Dolphin King*?

3–4 These questions check learners' understanding of the story by asking them to complete sentences and then to copy sentences that are true.

Answers

1 Arthur
2 ladybird, sheep, grasshopper
3 busy buzzing, jumping, gazed, started feeling, started going
4 Arthur was falling asleep.; The hippo was a cloud shape.; The hippo was in Arthur's dream.

Student's Book page 65

Spelling: suffixes

Revise the term 'suffix', with particular reference to –*ly*, and the learners' understanding of how adding a suffix to the end of word makes a new word. Encourage learners to give examples and ask others to either underline (if written) or say (if oral) the suffix used.

This activity focuses on adding a suffix –*ly* to a word to make a new word.

Write the following words on the board and ask the learners to look at the similarities and differences in each word.

> 'slow' – 'slowly'; 'quick' – 'quickly'; 'soft' – 'softly'; 'loud' – 'loudly'; 'nice' – 'nicely'; 'safe' – 'safely'; 'love' – 'lovely'

Highlight the part of each word that makes it different from its partner.

Establish the following with the learners:

- *ly* is a suffix.
- A suffix is a group of letters added to the end of a word to make a new word.

Write sentences, with a word missing, on the whiteboard and invite learners to say which word is missing.

Examples:

> You will be _____ in here.
> (safe, safely)
>
> He put the money away _____.
> (safe, safely)
>
> She spoke in a very _____ voice.
> (soft, softly)
>
> She spoke very _____. (soft, softly)

Note: Words with suffixes have more than one syllable and the learners should be encouraged to split words into syllables for spelling. Monitor where errors might occur, with the suffix or with the root word.

Ask the learners to write words with –*ly* to dictation

1–3 The learners do the activities on page 65

Dictation

Use these sentences to reinforce spellings of words with the suffix –*ly*.

- The car drove slowly along the street.
- She spoke clearly and loudly.
- He crossed the road safely.

Extension: Remind the learners, who have investigated the common suffix _–less_, that there are now three suffixes which they know and can use. Ask learners to give examples of these in sentences before they turn to PCM 23.

Weekly review

Use this rubric to assess learners' progress as they worked through the activities this week.

Level	Reading	Writing	Listening and speaking
■	This group read can read familiar text aloud with increased accuracy, fluency and expression.	This group understand how to add a suffix but need some support for spelling.	This group demonstrate attentive listening and attempt to express ideas in group situations.
●	This group is beginning to read aloud with increased accuracy, fluency and expression, taking some notice of punctuation including speech marks.	This group is beginning to use suffixes, with increased accuracy.	This group demonstrate attentive listening and attempt to express ideas clearly during any group/class discussion.
▲	This group read aloud with increased accuracy, fluency and expression, taking some notice of punctuation including speech marks.	This group can spell words with the suffix _–ly_. They can use the words when writing in sentences.	This group demonstrate attentive listening and are able to express ideas clearly during any group/class discussion.

Week 2

Student's Book pages 66–67

Workbook pages 43–45

Workbook page 43

Reading and writing
Before turning to the activity, use the text and ask learners to find and read the words that the characters say. For example:

page 1 What did Flora say?

page 3 What did the hippo say?

page 4 What did the ladybird say?

Discuss the use of speech marks in text, and how they show the exact words that the character says.

Write some simple sentences on the whiteboard and invite the learners to add the speech marks. It is a good idea to use a coloured pen for this so that the speech marks are easily seen.

Examples:
- Can I go to the park? asked Asif.
- I don't want to play, said Pam.
- Mum said, Do you want a drink?

In this activity learners find and write the name of the character who said each phrase.

Remind them that in the story the sentences will have speech marks round them to show that they are the words that the character said.

Answers
Arthur, Flora, hippo, Arthur, hippo, ladybird, grasshopper, grasshopper, Arthur, Flora

Student's Book page 66

Reading and thinking
This section focuses on comprehension of the story, and reinforces previous skills by using words from the story in a 'compound word' activity, and the use of capital letters at the beginning of proper names.

Revisit these by asking questions such as:
- What is a compound word?

- What word is made when 'down' and 'stairs' are joined? Similarly, for 'straw' and 'berry', 'moon' and 'light' and so on.
- What are the two words that make up 'screwdriver', 'bedroom', 'toothpaste'?

Recap with learners where capital letters are used in writing.

1 Learners answer questions by choosing the correct answer from a choice of two.

2 Learners are asked to write the two small words that make up each of four compound words.

3 Learners are asked to say why a capital letter is used at the beginning of the word 'Crazylegs'.

Reading and talking
The learners read the text and answer the questions.

Answers
1 Arthur, Arthur, ladybird
2 grass/hopper, lady/bird, butter/fly, Crazy/legs.
3 It is the name of the dancing competition (proper noun).

Workbook page 44
Reading
1 Learners match words with their meanings.

2 Learners choose, from a choice of two, the meaning that best matches 'They danced until their legs felt like jelly.'

Answers
1 jump – to leap; mumble – to speak quietly and not clearly; hop – to jump on one leg; competition – a contest; twirl – to turn around in a circle; grumble – to complain; bounce – to spring up; gaze – to stare at
2 They danced until their legs were very tired.

Workbook page 45
Sounds and spelling
1–2 Before learners learn to spell past tense verbs, it is important that they understand about the class of words described as verbs.

Sentences are made up of different types of words and each type has its own job to do in the sentence.

A **verb** is a doing or action word.

Invite learners to give examples of verbs.

Play oral games that require learners to change the tense from present to past and the reverse.

Examples:

Today I am painting. Yesterday I painted.

Today I am jumping. Yesterday I _____.

Yesterday I played. Today I am _____.

What are you doing? The learners could mime the action here.

A learner replies: I am washing the car.

I am reading a book.

What did you do yesterday?

A learner replies: I walked to the shops.

At this time, focus on the verbs where –ed is added to the root word to make the past tense.

Suggested words: 'rush', 'jump', 'mark', 'crack', 'play', 'bang', 'cool', 'drown', 'join', 'open', 'pull', 'lick', 'sail', 'crash'.

Note: It can be difficult for learners to remember to add the e when adding –ed as it is not always heard in speech. Another common mistake can be adding t to make the past tense, for example, 'jumpt'.

A mnemonic that might help here is:

> Never d, never t. Always add –ed.

Investigate words such as 'hunted', 'lifted', 'landed', 'mended', 'panted', 'shouted', 'painted' and 'toasted' where a second syllable can be heard.

Some of the words that describe 'dancing' at the Crazylegs Dancing Competition like 'dance', 'prance', 'bounce' are different in the past tense formation: 'dance'/'danced', 'prance'/'pranced', 'bounce'/'bounced'.

Investigate these words with the learners by asking them how the words changed to the past tense.

Dictation
- She locked the door of the shed.
- Jez helped to pack the case.
- He pushed the cart down the hill.
- The plane landed on the ground.
- The crowd shouted for the game to start.

Extension: Learners could investigate words in which the last consonant is doubled before adding –ed or –ing.

Examples: 'rob', 'robbed', 'robbing'; 'pat', 'patted', 'patting'; 'hop', 'hopped', 'hopping'; 'hug', 'hugged', 'hugging'.

Ask learners to read the words and say what they notice about them. Is there a pattern?

Help learners to deduce what the rule might be when adding *–ed* or *–ing* to words like 'hop'.

Answers
1 twirled, jumped, started, wanted, waited, pushed, banged, rested, crashed, parked, landed, played, melted, kicked
2 danced, pranced, bounced, grumbled

Student's Book page 67
Reading and writing
This activity provides further work on verbs.

1 Learners read about what happened at the Amazing Crazylegs Dancing Competition and write a list of the verbs.

2 Learners choose the correct verb to complete sentences to tell friends what they can do at the Crazylegs Dancing Competition.

3 Learners are asked to add *–ed* to verbs to make the past tense.

4 Learners choose two of the verbs and write a sentence for each.

Answers
1 danced, jumped, joined in, bounced, pranced, skipped, hopped, twirled
2 dance, jump, bounce, prance, skip, hop, twirl
3 rushed, played, pulled, jumped, pushed
4 Learners' own answers.

Weekly review
Use this rubric to assess learners' progress as they worked through the activities this week.

Level	Reading	Writing	Listening and speaking
■	This group can read and respond to question words. They need some support to find answers when the questions are not literal.	This group need support to use the past and present tenses accurately in spoken and written form.	This group do not always articulate clearly, making it difficult for others to understand at times.
●	This group can read and respond to question words. They can find answers to most questions by reading a section of text.	This group understand and use the past and present tenses well in spoken language, but are not always accurate in their use in the written form.	This group demonstrate attentive listening and articulate word endings clearly.
▲	This group can read and respond to question words. They can find answers to questions by reading a section of text.	This group understand and use the past and present tenses accurately (if not always consistently).	This group demonstrate attentive listening and articulate word endings clearly.

Week 3

Student's Book pages 68–70

Workbook pages 46–47

Workbook page 46
Writing
Before learners turn to the activity, ask them to look at the speech bubbles in turn and to find the words, contained in the speech bubble, in the text. Tell them which page to find each quote on.

For example:
- I don't want to go to sleep. page 1
- Where do you want to go? page 3
- Come with me. page 4
- The winner is … ARTHUR! page8
- Time to get up. page 10

78

Discuss speech marks with the learners, how they are written and where they are positioned. Discuss other punctuation like commas, question marks and exclamation marks.

Model and give the learners practice in adding punctuation to written sentences. For example:

I am hungry said Jen.

Where is my book asked Harry.

Answers
"I don't want to go to sleep," grumbled Arthur.
"Where do you want to go?" the hippo asked.
"Come with me," said the ladybird.
The grasshopper said, "… and the winner is … ARTHUR!"
"I have to go now," he said.

Student's Book page 68

Writing
1–2 This section focuses on words that can make dialogue more interesting in stories.

Ask learners to read page 1 again. Focus on the words 'mumbled' and 'grumbled' and ask learners what difference these words make to how the characters would speak.

Ask learners to experiment with reading page 1 aloud with good expression and characterisation to suit the words 'mumbled' and 'grumbled'.

Discuss with learners words like 'moaned', 'sighed', 'shouted', 'yelled', 'replied', 'whispered', 'groaned', and so on and sentences that they could be used in.

Discuss how using different words makes their writing more interesting to the reader.

Speaking and listening
Tell learners they are going to listen to a traditional African lullaby. Explain that a lullaby is a song that people sing to babies to get them to go to sleep. Play the audio or read the lullaby in an expressive way for the class.

Give learners time to read and practise the verse before asking individuals to recite it for the class.

Answers
1 asked, moaned, whispered, yelled, answered
2 Learners' own answers.

Student's Book page 69

Sounds and spelling
1 Write the following sentence on the whiteboard: 'They danced and bounced and pranced at the place where no one sleeps.'

Ask learners to read the sentence aloud and comment on anything they notice about some of the words. Highlight 'danced', 'bounced', 'pranced' and 'place' if necessary.

Elicit from the learners what these words have in common (a soft *c*). The letter *c* sounds like the sound *s*.

There are a number of rules in the English language for spelling words with soft *c* which should be taught at a later stage. However, at the moment, it is important that learners recognise when reading, the two sounds that the letter can represent.

2 Before learners turn to the activity, draw their attention to words like 'ace', 'face', 'pace', 'lace', 'race', 'ice', 'dice', 'rice', 'mice', 'price', 'twice' and show how onset and rhyme helps the learners to spell the words.

In these words the soft *c* is found at the end of words . If the *ss* sound is at the end of a word it is usually spelt *ce*.

Take opportunities to highlight these words when they arise in text.

Answers
2 face, lace, pace, race; price, lice, dice, mice, rice, nice

Reading and writing
1 Learners change the underlined word in sentences for a word with a similar meaning from the box above.

2 Learners write the words in alphabetical order.

3 Learners write the words again and mark the syllables.

Extension: Use PCM 24 to give additional practise with the soft 'c' sound.

Answers
1 gazing, amazing, crazy
2 amazing, crazy, gazing
3 a/maz/ing, cra/zy, gaz/ing

Student's Book page 70

Reading and writing

This section focuses on the Amazing Crazylegs Dancing Competition. Learners design a poster advertising the competition, interview Arthur and write a report for the local newspaper.

1 Ask learners to read the captions and then discuss with them how they are written and why they are written in the way they are

Discuss style, colour, size of lettering, and the short 'punchy' style that the phrases and sentences are written in.

2 Before learners turn to question 2, discuss with them what information should be on the poster. Learners could make a rough plan of content and layout of their poster before designing their actual poster.

Support: Work with a group to help with planning, helping with content and layout.

Speaking and listening

Before learners turn to the activity, discuss the role of a reporter and what sort of questions he/she might ask.

For example: Why did you enter the competition? How many people entered the competition? How did you feel when you won? Have you won a competition like that before? Was there a big audience watching?

Encourage learners to think about how the reporter might speak and how Arthur might speak. How would the excitement of Arthur's win influence the way he would speak?

Each learner should have a turn of being the reporter and a turn of being Arthur.

Writing

Learners now use the information from their interview to write a short report about the Crazylegs Dancing Competition. Remind them to think of a good heading for their writing.

Workbook page 47

Writing

1–2 The last activity in this unit asks learners to draw a picture and write about an imaginary dream.

Ask learners to work in pairs to talk about an imaginary dream before inviting individuals to tell their dream to their peers. Learners then draw and write their own dream story.

Weekly review

Use this rubric to assess learners' progress as they worked through the activities this week.

Level	Reading	Writing	Listening and speaking
■	This group show some awareness that texts have different purposes and with support can identify features of posters.	This group need support to plan and use simple organisational devices when designing a poster.	This group become quite animated in role-play situations and are becoming more aware that speakers speak in different ways.
●	This group show awareness that texts have different purposes and can identify features of posters with minimal teacher support.	With support at the planning stage this group can use simple organisational devices when designing a poster.	In role-play situations this group are becoming more confident in using different voices.
▲	This group show awareness that texts have different purposes and can identify features of posters.	This group can plan and use simple organisational devices when designing a poster.	In role-play situations this group show awareness that speakers speak in different ways.

End of unit assessment

Hand out PCM 25 to the learners and let them work independently to complete it under test conditions. Allow them to refer back to the story in their books if they need to, but do not allow them to collaborate on the work. Check the answers and note which learners need additional support at this stage.

Unit 8 The Pot of Gold

Unit overview

The Pot of Gold is a version of a folk tale from Ireland written by Julia Donaldson, who also wrote *Worm Looks for Lunch*, which the learners worked with in Unit 3.

As learners work through the unit, they will read aloud, retell and talk about events and characters in a story. They will also do some research to find out more about an author and compare the two (or more) stories they have read by the same author.

Learners will have opportunities to develop hearing and identifying phonemes in words and to segment and blend phonemes to spell and read words in isolation and embedded in text.

They will have opportunities to read high frequency words and extend the range of words recognised on sight.

Reading	Writing	Listening and speaking
2R06 Read aloud with increased accuracy, fluency and expression;	2W03 Begin to reread own writing aloud to check for sense and accuracy;	2SL1 Recount experiences and explore possibilities;
2R07 Begin to read with fluency and expression, taking some notice of punctuation, including speech marks;	2W05 Use the structures of familiar poems and stories in developing own writing;	2SL3 Articulate clearly so that others can hear;
2R10 Discuss the meaning of unfamiliar words encountered in reading;	2W06 Plan writing through discussion or by speaking aloud;	2SL6 Attempt to express ideas precisely, using a growing vocabulary;
2Rx3 Find answers to questions by reading a section of text;	2Wa2 Choose interesting words and phrases, e.g. in describing people and places;	2SL7 Listen carefully and respond appropriately, asking questions of others;
2Ri2 Identify and describe story settings and characters, recognising that they may be from different times and places;	2Wa4 Begin to use dialogue in stories;	2SL8 Demonstrate 'attentive listening' and engage with another speaker
2Ri3 Make simple inferences from the words on the page, e.g. about feelings;	2Wt1 Structure a story with a beginning, middle and end;	
2Rw1 Comment on some vocabulary choices, e.g. adjectives;	2Wp1 Write in clear sentences using capital letters, full stops and question marks;	
2Rw2 Talk about what happens at the beginning, in the middle or at the end of a story;	2Wp3 Use mainly simple and compound sentences, with 'and'/'but' to connect ideas; 'because' may begin to be used in a complex sentence;	
2Rx1 Read and respond to question words, e.g. 'what', 'where', 'when', 'who', 'why';	2Wp4 Use past and present tenses accurately (if not always consistently);	
2Ri1 Predict story endings	2Ws2 Apply knowledge of phonemes and spelling patterns in writing independently as well as when writing sentences from memory dictated by the teacher;	
	2Ws3 Secure the spelling of high frequency words and common irregular words	

Related resources

- Slideshow 8: *The Pot of Gold*
- Audio file: *The Pot of Gold*
- PCM 26: Speech bubbles
- PCM 27: Question words
- PCM 28: End of unit assessment

Introducing the unit

Show images of traditional story settings and discuss them with the class. Ask learners to identify features that are common to many traditional stories, for example, a cottage deep in the woods, children living on their own, strange creatures, talking plants and/or animals and so on. Discuss who lives in each house. Let learners suggest answers based on external clues before you move inside for further clues.

Talk about other fairy tales and ask learners to share their favourites.

Remind learners about a previous traditional tale that they read, *The Dolphin King*. Ask them to define in their terms what they understand by the words 'traditional tale'. Reinforce that it is a popular story that has been passed on in the spoken form, from one generation to the next, before ever being written down. There are often different versions of the story.

Week 1

Student's Book pages 71–76

Workbook page 48

Student's Book pages 71–75

Listening and speaking

Tell learners they are going to work in pairs to study the cover of a book and then to read it. Explain that they are to read and follow the instructions carefully.

1 Walk around as the learners start working and check that they know what they have to do. Give them enough time to complete the discussion and the reading.

Draw the learners together after some time and invite them to contribute to a class discussion about the book cover.

Ask learners to justify their answers, for example: What tells the learner that the two characters on the front cover are grumpy/arguing/not speaking to each other?

2 Ask learners to look at the picture and ask which part of the book it has come from. Discuss the word 'blurb' and its meaning.

Learners should then be given time to discuss what is asked in question 2 before drawing them together for a class discussion.

Discuss how illustrations can help with reading 'tricky' words, for example, 'arguing'.

Ask learners to look closely at the picture of the little man and remember that the story is a traditional tale from Ireland.

Tell the learners that Irish folk tales often have a character like this called a 'leprechaun'. He is usually shown as a little man, wearing a green coat and hat.

The stories usually involve a pot of gold at the end of a rainbow.

Extension: Learners could research other mythical creatures like leprechauns.

3 Ask learners to read the story in pairs, quietly and independently. Monitor, asking individual learners to read aloud. Check that they are using a range of strategies to tackle unknown words: looking at the pictures, sounding out words, using context and grammatical clues, reading on and rereading.

For example:

- There are a number of compound words in the story: 'doorstep', 'something', 'someone', 'everyone', 'downstairs', 'upstairs'. Are the learners breaking the words into their two component parts to help with reading?
- Are the learners able to read words with *–ing*, like 'arguing', 'gleaming', 'shouting', 'making'. If there is a problem, for example with 'gleaming', ask: Which part of the word is causing the problem? Is it *–ing* or the long vowel phoneme *ea*?

Use ongoing assessments like these to determine next steps for individual or groups of learners.

After the learners have had an opportunity to read the story themselves, draw the class together and invite individuals to read while others follow the text.

Highlight and praise strategies used to decipher any new or unfamiliar words.

Spend as much time as necessary with individuals or groups to ensure accurate decoding.

Spend some time ensuring the learners' understanding of the text before moving on to the Student's Book and the Workbook activities by asking questions like:

- What did Sandy and Bonny agree about when the little man took two gold coins out of his pocket?
- Why did Sandy run home to fetch a big pot?
- Why did Bonny not want Sandy to go for the gold coins during the day?

Discuss the moral of the story. Why couldn't Sandy and Bonny find the gold? Has the little man taught Sandy and Bonny a lesson?

Tell the class that this story was written by Julia Donaldson, the same person who wrote *Worm Looks For Lunch*. Spend some time talking about the two stories and how they are similar/different. Some learners may have read other stories by Julia Donaldson, if so, let them talk about these as well. (*The Gruffalo* is probably the best known.)

Use Julia Donaldson's own website http://www.juliadonaldson.co.uk/ to find out more about her and to prepare a class display about her work. Encourage learners to read the synopses of different titles and to listen to the audio-versions using the given links. There are also some printable activity sheets that you might find useful.

Workbook page 48

Writing
Before the learners turn to the activity, spend a short time asking them to choose a word to describe some objects, for example: a ball, a piece of rag, a baby, a lion, a car, a story. Encourage the learners to choose interesting adjectives (and not just colours) such as, 'a burst ball', 'a dirty rag', 'a gorgeous baby', 'a fierce lion', 'a rusty car', 'a fantastic story'.

The learners should then turn to page 48 and write a phrase with an adjective for each picture. One has been done for them.

Student's Book page 76

Writing
1 Discuss with the learners the meaning of the word 'description' and what should be included in a description.

Model writing a description by using a character from another book, before the learners write their descriptions of Sandy or Bonny.

Extension: Learners could make 'Lost' posters for a lost toy. The poster should include a picture and a written description of the toy.

2 Learners answer questions about the first part of the story. Remind them to answer the questions in sentences.

3 Learners read a passage about the old man and write the adjectives that describe him and what he wore.

4–5 Before learners turn to these questions, spend some time discussing possible adjectives that would change the description of the man.

Extension: Learners could extend the passage and add more adjectives to the passage, for example: There on the broken doorstep of the spooky house stood …

Answers
1 Learners' own descriptions.
2 everything, evening, a little man
3 little, green, ragged
4 Learners' own answers.
5 Learners' own drawings.

Weekly review
Use this rubric to assess learners' progress as they worked through the activities this week.

Level	Reading	Writing
■	This group can identify and describe story characters.	This group can change a piece of text by choosing different adjectives when they are given a list.
●	This group understand the concept of a traditional story. They can identify and describe story characters.	This group can change a piece of text by adding different and interesting adjectives of their own.
▲	This group understand the concept of a traditional story. They can identify and describe story characters, recognising that they are fictional.	This group can extend a piece of text by adding adjectives to make it more interesting.

Week 2

Student's Book pages 77–78

Workbook pages 49–51

Workbook page 49

Writing

Have some comic strips available to show learners how they are written.

Turn to Workbook page 48 and invite learners to suggest what the speech bubbles might contain. Look at each frame individually with them and work through what the conversation would have been.

For example: Frame 1 Read the text and tell the learners that what is written in the speech bubbles needs to be connected to the text.

And so 'Too many sheep' would be written in the speech bubble for Bonny and 'Not enough sheep' would be written in the speech bubble for Sandy.

Frame 2 One evening there was a tap at the door.

What might the little man have said when Bonny opened the door?

What might Bonny have said?

Frame 3 The little man asked to stay for two nights, and then what did he say?

Sandy and Bonny answered together. What did they say?

Frame 4 What did the little man say when he was in his room?

What did Bonny say in reply?

Once you have done the work orally, let learners complete the task on their own or in pairs.

Support: Use PCM 26 to support some learners with this activity. It allows them to manipulate the speech bubbles and work out where to put them.

Student's Book page 77

Reading and writing
This section continues to focus on direct speech. This time the learners copy and complete sentences by adding the words that the character said within speech marks.

Speaking and listening
Learners work in pairs to discuss a time when they argued with someone. Draw them together and use one pair to highlight some points. For example:

- What caused the argument?

- Was the cause of the argument worth arguing about?

- Should they have argued or was there another way to resolve the dispute?

- How did they feel after the argument?

Writing
Learners now write about a time when they argued with someone. They can choose how best to present this piece of writing – some may choose a diary entry, others may draw a comic. Encourage a range of options.

Workbook page 50

Reading
1 Learners match words from the story to their meanings.

2 Learners draw three coins that they know.

Have some coins available and discuss size, colour and value before the learners draw three coins.

Student's Book page 78

Reading and writing
1 This question focuses on the learners' understanding of the story by asking them to read sentences and then to write the sentences that are true.

Remind the learners that they must be able to find evidence in the text to say that a sentence is true.

2 The second part of the activity focuses on using conjunctions to connect pairs of simple sentences.

Write pairs of simple sentences on the whiteboard and tell the learners to choose 'and' or 'but' to join the sentences into one.

It is good practice to read each sentence aloud and then to read the first sentence aloud again in a way that will help the leasrners anticipate what comes next from the intonation of your voice.

Examples:

- I went to the shops. I bought some milk.

- I stayed in the house. I watched television.

- I went to the park. I played football.

- Mum shouted my name. I didn't hear her.

- I looked in the tin. It was empty.

- I fell. I didn't hurt myself.

Then move on to look at sentences that could be joined by 'because'.

For example:

- You should take an umbrella. It might rain.

84

- Don't drink the water. It is dirty.
- Dad bought a new bike. His old one was broken.

Learners should then complete the activity in writing.

Support: Support individuals or small groups by reading the sentences with them and using your voice to help them anticipate the conjunction to use.

Answers
1 True: Sandy wanted to buy more sheep.; Bonny wanted to buy new clothes.; Sandy laughed when Bonny threw water all over the little man.
2 and, because, because, but, and

Workbook page 51

Reading
Before learners turn to this activity, ask them to reread the story. Discuss strategies for putting the sentences in order.

- Read all the sentences first, before writing any numbers.
- Look for possible clues – is there a sentence that is obviously first? Think back to the story. What happened first? Similarly, is there a sentence that is obviously last?
- What had to happen to make something else happen? For example: Sandy and Bonny had to look for the gold before they couldn't find it.
- Look for words like 'then' and 'next'. These words mean that something else had to have happened before that part of the story.
- Read and reread. Is the order making sense? Check with the text if necessary.

Answers
2, 5, 1, 7, 3, 6, 8, 4

Weekly review

Use this rubric to assess learners' progress as they worked through the activities this week.

Level	Reading	Writing
■	This group can sequence events when they can read and manipulate the text.	This group can identify and use the features of a comic strip and with support can 'write' a dialogue.
●	This group have a good understanding of the sequence of events in a story. They can read and with minimal support then sequence events.	This group can identify and use the features of a comic strip and with minimal support can a write a dialogue.
▲	This group have a good understanding of the sequence of events in a story. They can read and sequence events accurately.	This group can identify and use the features of a comic strip to write a write a dialogue.

Week 3

Student's Book pages 79–80

Workbook pages 52–53

Student's Book page 79

Reading and writing
1–2 In question 1 learners use words from the story in a different context. Question 2 focuses on question words.

Elicit from the learners the difference between a question and an answer. Discuss how we can tell the difference between a question and an answer.

Ask learners to work in pairs asking and answering questions. After their conversations, ask learners to note down the question words they used before inviting them to share the words they used with their peers. Write words such as 'who', 'what', 'where', 'when', 'why' and 'how' on the whiteboard. Invite learners to look for similarities/differences between the words.

Discuss any tricky parts of the word and ways to help learners remember the spellings. 'Who' and 'how' are often confused. Alert learners to their spellings and encourage them to think of ways that may help them remember the spellings. The mnemonic 'We Had Oranges' may help some learners remember how to spell 'who'.

Learners should then complete the activity.

3 Learners are asked to find and write the compound words in question 3.

Dictation
Use these or similar sentences to reinforce spelling of question words.

- What is the title of the book?
- Why are you waiting for the bus?
- When will you come to my house?
- Where are you going?
- Who will be at the party?

Answers
1 temper, argued, gleaming, evening, hunted
2 who, what, where, when, how
3 doorbell, today, supermarket

Workbook page 52
Writing
Before learners write a list of questions for an interview with Sandy and Bonny, ask them to tell you the six question words from the previous activity. Write the words on the whiteboard and remind learners that they should use them when writing their questions.

Use PCM 27 to give the learners further practice in writing question words and structuring interview questions.

Student's Book page 80
Writing
In this activity learners are asked to use the structure of *The Pot of Gold* to write their own story.

1–3 Learners look at pictures, which tell a different story.

The pictures show Sandy and Bonny as happy children who make the little man feel welcome by giving him food, playing a game with him, showing him to his room, before saying goodbye after breakfast.

Learners write a story using the pictures as a guide before writing an ending for the story.

Before learners turn to writing the story, give them time to work in pairs to plan their story by discussing the points in question 1.

Draw the class together and discuss how their stories will be different from *The Pot of Gold*. The characters will be different and so there should be a different ending.

Agree targets with the learners about what they should include in their stories. These should match skills you have been working on. Do not give too many targets at once.

For example:

- a good beginning for the story
- good descriptive words
- sentences with capital letters and full stops
- spelling known words accurately.

Workbook page 53
Reading and writing
1 Learners write the words in alphabetical order.

2 Learners complete the word search.

Weekly review
Use this rubric to assess learners' progress as they worked through the activities this week.

Level	Writing	Listening and speaking
■	This group can write a short description using interesting words to describe characters.	This group discuss their ideas and with support can use them to plan their story.
●	This group can write a longer description using interesting words and phrases to describe characters.	This group discuss their ideas and extend them in discussion and are beginning to make use of discussion points in story writing.
▲	This group can write a detailed description using interesting words and phrases to describe characters. They can write with a variety of sentence types.	This group discuss their ideas and extend them in discussion. They make good use of discussion points in story writing.

End of unit assessment
Use PCM 28 to assess learners' abilities to write a detailed description using given adjectives and additional ones of their own.

Learners should hand in their descriptions for marking. Take note of which learners need additional support in this area.

86

Unit 9 People who help us

Unit overview

As learners work through the unit they will develop an understanding of how to use a non-fiction book and how it differs from a story book. They will learn that texts have different purposes and be able to identify features of a non-fiction text. At the same time, they will deal with instruction text and reinforce earlier work on dictionaries, glossaries and indexes.

Learners will need to find factual information from text, photographs, captions and charts and use this to answer questions and also to develop their own writing.

They will learn how to use simple organisational devices in non-fiction writing.

Reading	Writing	Listening and speaking
2R06 Read aloud with increased accuracy, fluency and expression; 2R03 Identify syllables and split familiar compound words into parts; 2R04 Extend the range of common words recognised on sight; 2R05 Begin to develop likes and dislikes in reading and listening to stories drawing on background information and vocabulary provided; 2R07 Begin to read with fluency and expression, taking some notice of punctuation, including speech marks; 2R10 Discuss the meaning of unfamiliar words encountered in reading; 2Rx1 Read and respond to question words, e.g. 'what', 'where', 'when', 'who', 'why'; 2Rx3 Find answers to questions by reading a section of text; 2Rx4 Find factual information from different formats, e.g. charts, labelled diagrams; 2Rv1 Show some awareness that texts have different purposes; 2Rv2 Identify general features of known text types	2W03 Begin to reread own writing aloud to check for sense and accuracy. 2W06 Plan writing through discussion or by speaking aloud; 2Wa1 Develop stories with a setting, characters and a sequence of events; 2Wa3 Build and use collections of interesting and significant words; 2Wa5 Use features of chosen text type; 2Wa6 Write instructions and recount events and experiences; 2Wt4 Use a variety of simple organisational devices in non-fiction, e.g. headings, captions; 2Wp1 Write in clear sentences using capital letters, full stops and question marks; 2Wp5 Begin to vary sentence openings, e.g. with simple adverbs; 2Wp6 Write with a variety of sentence types; 2Ws2 Apply knowledge of phonemes and spelling patterns in writing independently as well as when writing sentences from memory dictated by the teacher; 2Ws3 Secure the spelling of high frequency words and common irregular words	2SL3 Articulate clearly so that others can hear; 2SL6 Attempt to express ideas precisely, using a growing vocabulary; 2SL7 Listen carefully and respond appropriately, asking questions of others; 2SL8 Demonstrate 'attentive listening' and engage with another speaker

Related resources

- Slideshow 9: People who help us
- PCM 29: Compound words
- PCM 30: End of unit assessment

Introducing the unit

The focus in this unit is on firefighters and the work they do, but there are many other people in communities who help others. Begin this unit by making a large circle on the whiteboard with the words 'People who help us' in the centre. Have a brainstorming session with the class and ask them to call out the professions (or names) of people who help others in your community.

Once you have a number of contributions, spend some time talking about how these different people help the community.

Another alternative is to prepare a set of situations in which people need help, for example: a traffic accident, a bush fire, a lost child, someone has fallen and broken a limb, a thief has stolen a handbag, there are animals blocking the road, and so on. Learners should suggest where best to get help in the given situations.

Week 1

Student's Book pages 81–85

Workbook pages 54–55

Student's Book pages 81–83

If you have it available, show the class the front cover of *Fire! Fire!* and discuss whether it is a fiction or a non-fiction book.

Ask learners to look at the lettering on the front of the fire engine. (If you do not have *Fire! Fire!* available, an image of a fire engine will do). What do they notice about it? Ask if any of learners know why it is written in that way? Do they think it is necessary to have it written in reverse (mirror writing)? How do drivers know that a fire engine is approaching behind them? (siren, flashing lights)

What should drivers do if a fire engine or other rescue service vehicle (ambulance, police car) is approaching behind them?

Give learners the opportunity to use mirrors to see how writing looks when you look at it using a mirror.

Ask learners to look at page 81 and to look at the pictures, read the captions and the text.

Discuss the different good points about fire, reminding learners that an adult must always be present whenever children are near a fire – it can be very dangerous!

Ask learners what is dangerous about going too close to fire.

Write the words 'giant' and 'dangerous' on the whiteboard and ask the learners to read the words. What do they notice about the words?

Note: A soft *g* sounds like *j* as in 'jar'. A soft *g* is usually followed by an *e* as in 'gem', an *i* as in 'giraffe' or a *y* as in 'gym'. Some words starting with *gi*– and *ge*– don't have the *j* sound, for example, 'get', 'girl', 'gift', 'give'.

Ask learners to read the rest of the book (pages 82–83), monitoring that they read all the information on the page, including captions and labels.

Follow on by asking questions to ensure that the learners know how to use a non-fiction book and how to find information.

Examples:

- Show me the pages that you would find information about modern firefighting.
- Show me where you would find out about firefighters who fight fires in different countries.
- Find the page that tells us how firefighters fight fires in forests.

Workbook page 54

Sounds and spelling

Before learners turn to the activity, write the words 'giant' and 'dangerous' on the whiteboard and ask learners about what they had talked about previously – the soft *g*. Tell them that some words that they will meet in reading start with a soft *g*, like 'giant'.

Write the following words on the board and ask the learners to read them, reminding them that they start with a soft *g*: 'gem', 'gentle', 'gerbil', 'generous', 'ginger', 'giraffe', 'giant', 'gym'.

Discuss the words and their meanings before the learners turn to the activity on page 55.

Extension: Some learners could investigate the sound *j* at the end of words and how it is written.

Examples: 'age', 'cage', 'page', 'stage', 'wage', 'cabbage'.

Note: Tell learners the mnemonic rhyme: 'No English word can end in *j*. This is a rule you must obey.'

Note: Words like 'Haj' (from Arabic) and 'Raj' (from Hindi) which are used in the English speaking world are exceptions.

Student's Book page 84

Reading and writing
Ask learners to read page 81 again before completing the activities.

1 Learners choose words from the box to complete the sentences.

2 Learners find words from page 81 that rhyme with the words in the box.

3 Before turning to the activity, give learners time to look at page 81 again, read the text, look at the map, the pictures and the captions. Then ask them to say what information they found out from these pages.

Ask learners to read the names of the countries shown, including the UK and USA asking what the letters stand for. They may remember from the Olympics topic that the UK was referred to as GBR. What did that stand for?

Ask learners to point to the country that they live in, on the map. Is it labelled? If not, do they know where it is on a map? Ask learners to name some other countries that they know. Do they know anyone who lives in another country? If so, what country?

The learners should now answer the questions.

Answers
1 warm, light, cook, fireworks, dangerous, firefighters
2 fire, cook, make, why, light
3 United Kingdom, United States (of) America, learners' own answers

Student's Book page 85

Reading and writing
1 Learners match the words to make pairs of words that have similar meanings.

2 Learners write two sentences.

3 Learners look at the first picture on page 82 and list the items of clothing and equipment that the firefighters have.

Answers
1 dangerous and hazardous, trained and prepared, amusement and pleasure
2 Learners' own sentences.
3 Learners own lists. They may use their own words to describe the items.

Listening and speaking
Before learners work in pairs, ask them to read page 82 again. They should then work in pairs and, using the information that they have read and the pictures as a prompt, talk about:

• the different places that firefighters put out fires

• the different places that fires could start on land

• things that might cause fires on land.

Tell learners that they should choose one of the topics to tell their peers about.

Writing
Learners write sentences about one of the places that firefighters put out fires and then illustrate the sentences.

After these activities, learners could work together to make a large picture of a firefighter wearing the uniform of the country that they live in. The picture should then be labelled to show the items of clothing.

Extension: Learners could research the different types of vehicles used by the fire service and present their findings orally or as a poster to their peers.

Workbook page 55

Reading and writing
Learners match the names of items of clothing and equipment to their meanings.

Remind learners to read all the words and meanings before starting the matching activity.

Support: Support any learners who may find difficulty with decoding, to allow you to assess if they understand the meanings of the words.

Weekly review

Use this rubric to assess learners' progress as they worked through the activities this week.

Level	Reading	Listening and speaking
■	This group can find information from maps and pictures but need some support to find information from text.	This group can attempt to express ideas clearly when presenting to the class.
●	This group can find factual information from different formats, including text, maps, pictures and captions.	This group can attempt to express ideas clearly, using a growing vocabulary, when presenting to the class.
▲	This group can independently find factual information from different formats, including text, maps, pictures and captions.	This group can vary talk and expression to gain and hold the listener's attention when presenting to the class.

Week 2

Student's Book pages 86–87

Workbook page 56

Student's Book page 86

Reading and writing

Learners are asked to copy and complete a passage about fire engines and firefighters (taken from *Fire! Fire!*). The words are not provided and the learners need to work out what words to use.

Remind learners to read their work, checking that it makes sense.

When they are sure that it makes sense they should check it against page 82.

Answers
Possible answers are: wail, flash; the fire; water; hoses, hosepipes

Support: Work with a small group and read page 82 with them before discussing what words should be used to complete the sentences. Learners should then complete the task using the text as reference if necessary.

Speaking and listening

1 Before having a discussion with the class as a whole, give learners time to talk about:

- what can cause fires to start in houses
- what they should do if they notice a fire starting in a house.

Draw the class together, inviting learners to say what they have been discussing, highlighting the main causes of fires starting in the home.

Then move on to talk about what they should do if a) they are in a house when a fire starts and b) if they see a fire in a house from outside.

Learners should then design safety posters.

Discuss with learners what pictures and what kind of words would be on the poster, for example: 'DON'T LEAVE CANDLES NEAR CURTAINS', 'IT ONLY TAKES SECONDS FOR …'

2 Learners are asked to act out a situation where one is making a phone call to report a fire and the other is receiving the call.

Talk about the number they would call, and discuss if it is the same number for any other emergency service. Discuss how important it is only to call this number in a real emergency, and why it should never be called unless it is an emergency.

Talk about how the learners would speak on the phone. Would they speak in the same way as they speak to friend or relative on the telephone? Why not?

Writing

Before moving to the next section, discuss procedures for evacuating the school building should the fire alarm sound.

Ask learners to say in sequence what the members of the class should do if the fire alarm was sounded.

Learners should then write a list of instructions for evacuating the classroom.

1 Learners write the telephone number they would call to report a fire.

2 Learners write a list of important things to say when they phone to report a fire.

Workbook page 56

Sounds and spelling

1 Learners write small words that make up given compound words.

2 Learners mark the syllables in given words and say how many syllables are in each word.

In both of these, the words all come from the text *Fire! Fire!*

Answers
1 fire + fighters, fire + works, hose + pipes, blow + out, air+ ships
2 dan/ger/ous 3; heli/cop/ter 3; for/est 2; pow/er/ful 3

PCM 29 gives learners further practice in writing compound words and applying knowledge of phonemes.

Student's Book page 87

Reading and writing

1 Learners are asked to copy and complete a passage about forest fires (taken from *Fire! Fire!*). The words are not provided and learners need to work out what words to use.

Remind the learners to read their work, checking that it makes sense.

When they are sure that it makes sense they should check it against page 83.

Support: You should work with a small group and read page 11 with them before discussing what words should be used to complete the sentences. The learners should then complete the task using the text as reference if necessary

2 Question 2 is similar to question 1, but this time learners copy and complete a passage about a blowout. Reference page 82 of the text.

Speaking and listening
Before having a discussion with the class as a whole, give learners time to talk about:

*   why oil well fires are very dangerous to people
*   why fires spread quickly through forests
*   why helicopters must fly in low at forest fires.

Draw the class together, inviting learners to say what they have been discussing, highlighting the dangers of forest fires and how people need to be very careful when using matches/lighting barbeques in forest areas, and oil well fires.

Answers
1 possible answers: forests, helicopters, fly, grow
2 possible answers: fire, torch, blowout

Weekly review

Use this rubric to assess learners' progress as they worked through the activities this week.

Level	Writing	Listening and speaking
■	This group use features of a chosen text type by listing two or three important pieces of information.	This group extend their experiences and ideas through role play and show an awareness of appropriate voices for the situation.
●	This group use features of a chosen text type when listing important concise information.	This group extend their experiences and ideas through role play and show an awareness of appropriate voices and vocabulary for the situation.
▲	This group use features of a chosen text type effectively when listing important concise information.	This group extend their experiences and ideas through role play using appropriate vocabulary and tone of voice for the situation.

Week 3

Student's Book pages 88–90

Workbook pages 57–58

Student's Book page 88

Reading and writing

1 Learners copy and complete a passage about fire at sea (taken from *Fire! Fire!*). The words are not provided and the learners need to work out what words to use.

Remind learners to read their work, checking that it makes sense.

When they are sure that it makes sense they should check it against page 83.

Support: Monitor closely any learners that you have been supporting with this type of activity. This passage has more regularly phonetic words and high frequency words which should allow the learners to decode independently. This could act as a good assessment of progress.

2 Learners write a description of the fire boat shown on page 83.

Speaking and listening

Before having a discussion with the class as a whole, give learners time to talk about the clothing and equipment that firefighters need for fires at sea. Reference page 83.

Answers
1 jet skis, tanker, hoses

Workbook page 57

Reading

The learners match the beginning of sentences with their endings. The sentences all give information that has been read and discussed in *Fire! Fire!*

Answers
Fires can be dangerous.; The firefighters put out flames with jets of water from hosepipes.; Firefighters put out fires on land, at sea and from the air.; An oil well fire can burn like a huge, flaming torch.; Big oil tanker fires need fire boats with powerful hoses.; In the future, giant airships, robots and fast-fire cars might help to put put fires.

Student's Book page 89

Reading and writing

Before turning to the activity, have a selection of age appropriate non-fiction books with indexes available.

Highlight what an index in a book is. Ask learners to look at the index and elicit from them the key points that make an index.

- a list of topics, names or other information in a book
- the list is in alphabetical order
- page numbers are given to each thing on the list.

Ask learners to turn to the index page of a chosen book. Invite them to say a page number and what can be found on that page from the index of their chosen book.

Refer back to the image for the index of *Fire! Fire!* and work with them to use the index to help find the answers to the questions on page 89.

1 Learners should write the answers to the questions after the oral activities.

2 Learners choose two subjects from the index and write a sentence for each.

Discuss with the learners what a heading is and how it is written.

The learners should then write a title for the book and headings for the different sections of text on pages 81–83.

Answers
1 fires at sea (pages 10 and 11); drop water on them (page 12); oceans (page 10); fires on land, fires in buildings (pages 8 and 11); siren (page 8).

Workbook page 58

Reading

Use a selection of books with a glossary at the back of each to help learners understand what a glossary is, i.e. a list of unusual or difficult words and their meanings. A glossary is usually placed at the end of a book.

Before learners write the words for the meanings given, remind them to read all the words and the meanings first.

Extension: Ask learners to find and write a piece of information, using the glossary of other appropriate non-fiction books.

Answers
airships, fire boat, jet skis, oil well, sirens, water-bomb

Workbook page 59
Reading and writing
Learners write under four headings what information they have learnt about firefighters and firefighting. They should use the pictures to start but should then write as much other information as they can.

Student's Book page 90
Listening and speaking
Learners are asked to work in pairs to look at two pictures and talk about:

- why a fire engine might have a picture of an airplane on it
- why a fire engine is parked near the runway of an airport
- where fire hydrants are found and what they are for.

Draw the learners together for a class discussion.

Writing
Before learners turn to this activity, if possible, invite a firefighter into school to speak to the learners about his job.

Extension: Learners could write a letter inviting the firefighter to school. First discuss, with all learners, what should be in the letter to the firefighter.

Before the visit, learners should prepare questions that they would like to ask the firefighter.

1 After the visit, discuss what information the learners learnt from the firefighter and what points would be good to include in a job advertisement.

Ask the learners to write a 'Thank you' letter after the firefighter's visit.

2 Learners design and label a new machine for fighting fires in the future.

Weekly review
Use this rubric to assess learners' progress as they worked through the activities this week.

Level	Reading	Writing
■	This group understand the function of indexes and glossaries and can locate words in indexes.	This group need some support with planning and writing a job advertisement.
●	This group understand the function of indexes and glossaries and can locate words by initial letter in a given of books with minimal support.	This group need a little support with planning before writing a job advertisement.
▲	This group understand the function of indexes and glossaries and can locate words by initial letter in a variety of books.	This group can use a number of organisational devices to plan and write a job advertisement.

End of unit assessment

Use PCM 30 to assess whether or not learners have read and understood the information texts in this unit. Hand out the sheet and ask

learners to complete it independently. Once they have done so, let them compare their answers with others and discuss how to check and resolve any differences of opinion (by referring back to the texts).

Phonics a–e

❶ Write the correct word for each picture.

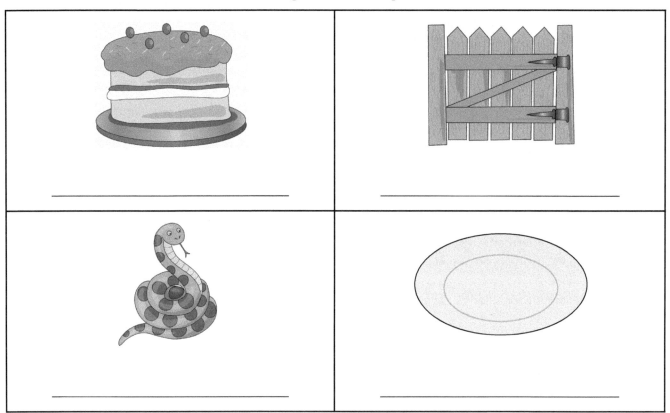

❷ Write rhyming words.

| t   sh   g   s   c   w |

bake	came	gave

❸ Complete and copy the sentences.

- Meera forgot to shut the _____.

- The _____ slid in the long grass.

Phonics ai, ay, a–e

❶ **Write the words for each picture in the correct list.**

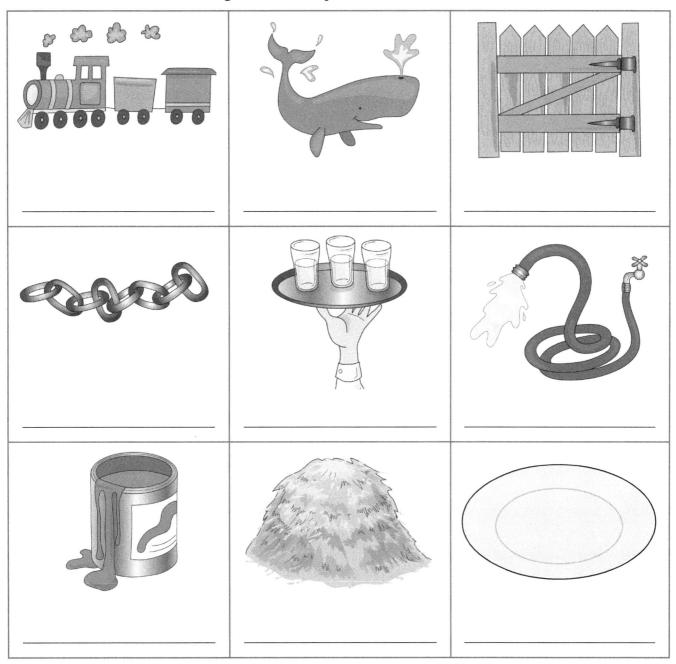

❷ **Write the words in rhyming lists.**

ai	ay	a–e

Phonics o–e

❶ Write the correct word for each picture.

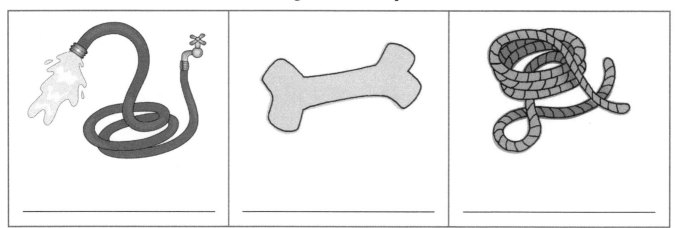

_____	_____	_____

❷ Write rhyming words.

w	h	p	r	sl

joke	sole	hope

❸ Complete and copy the sentences.

- The man put the _____ on the tap.

- The boy hid the _____ from the dog.

- The girl tied the _____ .

Compound words

❶ Join the two small words to make compound words.

foot	ball	*football*
black	bird	
down	stairs	
skate	board	
shoe	lace	
bed	room	
rain	bow	
dust	bin	
lady	bird	

❷ Complete the table.

greenhouse	*green + house*
postcard	
seaweed	
lamppost	
homework	
grandmother	
somebody	
someone	

Contractions

1 **Write each contraction in full.**

don't	do not
can't	
he's	

doesn't	
she's	
isn't	

2 **Use apostrophes to shorten and join together the underlined words. Write the sentences with the shortened words.**

- <u>He is</u> waiting for his dad by the bus stop.

  _____

- Ranvir <u>does not</u> want to see the film.

  _____

- <u>She is</u> going to play football, but he <u>is not</u> playing.

  _____

End of unit assessment

1 **Choose the best word for each sentence.**
Complete and copy the sentences.

| crackled   drip   squelch   clattered   smashed   honked |

- I can hear the _____ of the tap.

- The plates _____ on the floor when I
dropped them.

- The driver _____ the horn when he left the
bus stop.

- I heard the mud _____ when I walked in it.

- The sticks _____ on the fire as they burned.

- The glass _____ when the ball hit
the window.

Glossary words

❶ Cut out the words and arrange them in alphabetical order.

❷ The glossary of the book gives the following definitions. Cut out the definitions and match them to the correct words.

✂

stadium	ancient Greeks	discus
wreath	marathon	record

✂

a wooden disc with a metal rim used in a throwing competitions

a long-distance running race in which runners cover a distance of 42 kilometres

people who lived in Greece a very long time ago

the best performance officially recorded in a sport (fastest, furthest, heaviest, etc.)

the large venue where sporting events take place

a crown made of coiled leaves and branches

Phonics *ew*

❶ Read and draw.

a few pens	a screw and a screwdriver

❷ Write rhyming words.

| f   d   dr   fl |

new	blew

❸ Complete and copy the sentences.

| screw   grew |

- The _____ is in the tool box.

- The plant _____ well in the sun.

Phonics u–e

❶ Write the correct word for each picture.

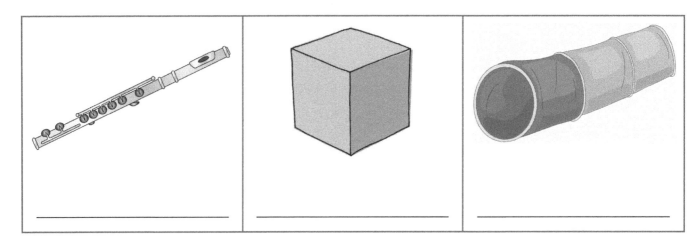

_____   _____   _____

❷ Write rhyming words.

c	fl	pr	t

brute	June

❸ Complete and copy the sentences.

June	flute	fuse

• The month after May is _____ .

• The plug has a _____ in it.

• I can play a tune on the _____ .

Write instructions

How to make an Olympic _____ .

What you need:

_____

_____

_____

_____

_____

Instructions:

_____

_____

_____

_____

_____

_____

_____

End of unit assessment

Medal Winner's Table Swimming at the 2012 Olympics

Women's 200 m freestyle		
Allison Schmitt	USA	🇺🇸
Camille Muffat	FRA	🇫🇷
Bronte Barratt	AUS	🇦🇺

Men's 200 m butterfly		
Chad le Clos	RSA	🇿🇦
Michael Phelps	USA	🇺🇸
Takeshi Matsuda	JPN	🇯🇵

Women's 100 m backstroke		
Missy Franklin	USA	🇺🇸
Emily Seebohm	AUS	🇦🇺
Aya Terakawa	JPN	🇯🇵

Men's 200 m backstroke		
Tyler Clary	USA	🇺🇸
Ryosuke Irie	JPN	🇯🇵
Ryan Lochte	USA	🇺🇸

❶ Who won the women's 200 m freestyle?

_____

❷ Who won the silver medal in the women's 100 m backstroke?

_____

❸ Who won the gold medal in the men's 200 m backstroke?

_____

❹ In which race did Australia win a silver medal?

_____

❺ In which race did the USA win a bronze medal?

_____

❻ List the medal winners of the men's 200 m butterfly.

_____

Food dictionary

❶ Write the names of the different foods in alphabetical order in the table below.

❷ Write a definition for each word. Use a dictionary to help you.

Word	Definition
carrot	a long pointed root vegetable, usually orange in colour

Phonics *ow* and *ou*

❶ Write the words

_____   _____   _____

❷ Complete and copy the sentences with ou words.

- A circle is a _____ shape.

- He fell on the _____ and hurt his leg.

- Mark had to _____ for help.

- The opposite of north is _____ .

- The cat chased the _____ .

End of unit assessment

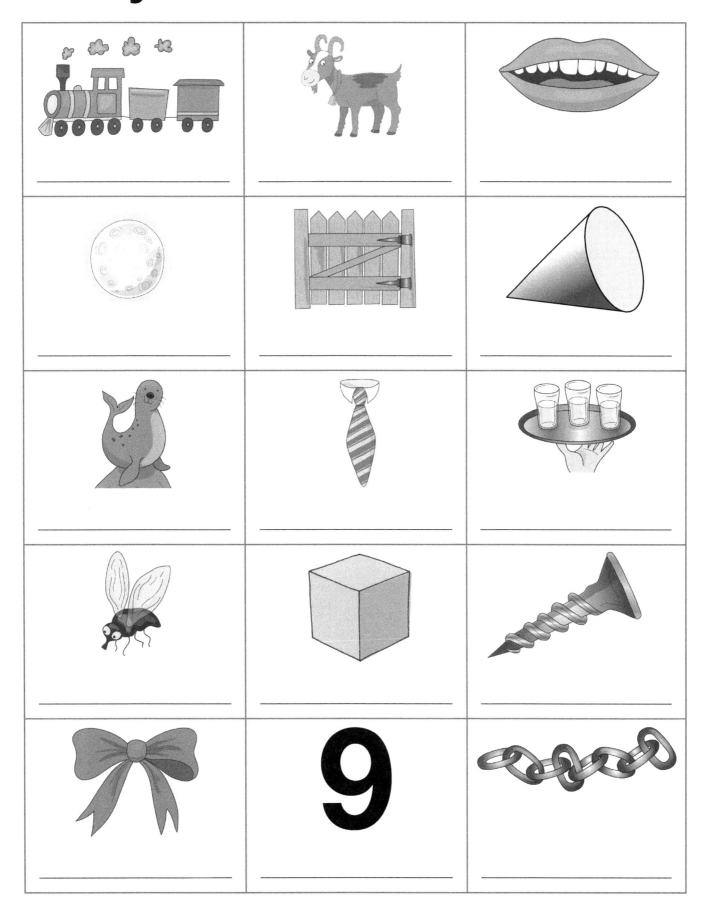

Prefixes

un– is a prefix.

healthy   un + healthy = unhealthy

1 **Choose prefixes from the sign below to make new words.**

Some words use more than one prefix.

Check the spellings of the new words in a dictionary.

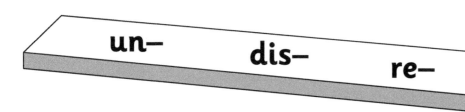

un–   dis–   re–

build	rebuild		use	
fill			tie	
trust			lock	
load			cycle	
lucky			obey	

End of unit assessment

❶ Add –ed to make new words. Write the words.

- bark + ed = _____
- bump + ed = _____
- melt + ed = _____
- ask + ed   = _____

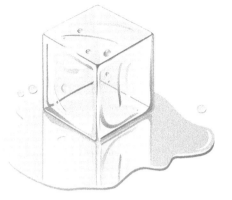

❷ Add a prefix to make new words. Write the words.

| un–   dis– |

- ____ + pack = _____
- ____ + obey = _____
- ____ + trust = _____
- ____ + well = _____

❸ Write two words that rhyme with each word.

- far   _____   _____
- corn   _____   _____

❹ Read and complete.

- We have the same mother and f_____ .
- She is my s_____ . I am h_____ brother.

Silent letters

1 Write the correct word to name each picture.

2 Circle the silent letter in each word.

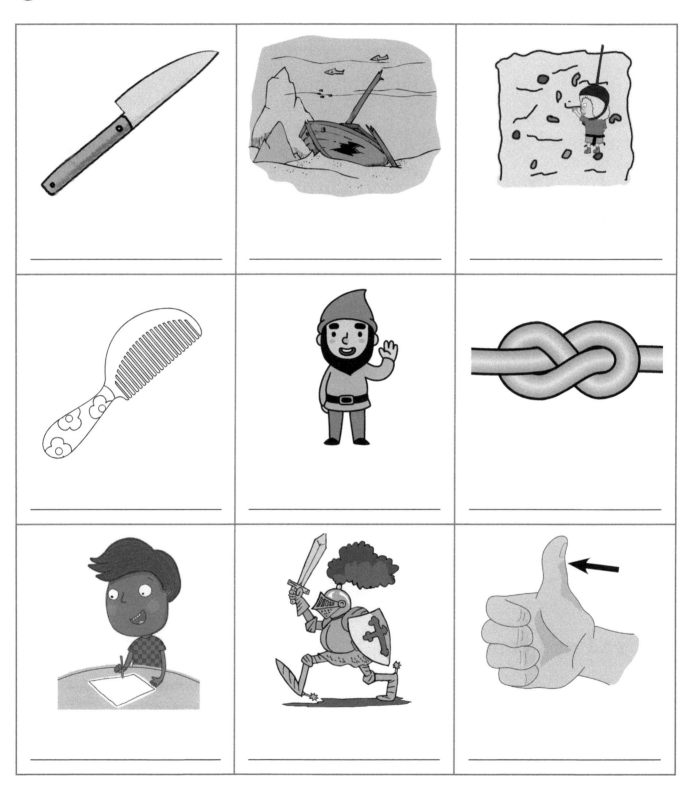

Sequencing

1 **Number the sentences in the correct order to match the story.**

The animal screamed and dived beneath the waves.	
A strange knight rose out of the waves.	
Jean promised never to hunt dolphins again.	
Jean hurled his spear at a dolphin.	
The knight carried Jean down to the bottom of the sea.	
Jean helped the dolphin king.	
Suddenly, a fierce storm blew up.	
There, the dolphin king was waiting.	

End of unit assessment

1 **Write a word to name each picture.**

 _____	 _____	 _____
 _____	a b c d e f g h i j k l m n o p q r s t u v w x y z _____	

2 **Add the suffix to make new words.**

- help + ful = _____

- play + ful = _____

- care + ful = _____

- hope + ful = _____

3 **Choose the best word to complete each sentence.**

> whispered   asked   shouted

- "Can I have something to eat?" _____ Akib.

- "Sh! The baby is sleeping," _____ Mum.

- "Come downstairs now!" _____ Fred.

Syllables

The word 'picnic' has
two syllables.

**❶ Write the words to show the syllables.
The first one has been done for you.**

carpet	*car / pet*
magnet	
planet	
velvet	
basket	

garden	
lemon	
window	
robin	
number	

❷ The syllables in the left column are in the wrong order.

Use them to write the words correctly.

Count the number of syllables in each word.

Syllables	Word	Number of syllables
pet/pup	*puppet*	*2*
bit/rab		
on/lem/ade		
na/na/ba		
ter/fly/but		
day/nes/Wed		

Phonics *ow*

❶ **Write the word for each picture.**
All the words have *ow* in them.

_____	_____	_____
_____	_____	_____

❷ **Read and complete the sentences using the words in the box.**

> towel   crow   crowd   tow

- A big _____ watched the game.

- A _____ is a type of bird.

- I dried my hands on a _____ .

- You need to _____ the car to the garage.

End of unit assessment

Use the chart to answer the questions.

	Sea	Jungle	Underground	Ice and snow
shark				
worm				
elephant				
dolphin				
polar bear				
tiger				
walrus				

- Which animals live in the jungle?

  _____

- Which habitat does the polar bear live in?

  _____

- Write the name of an animal that lives in the sea.

  _____

- Which creature lives underground?

  _____

Common suffixes

❶ Add the suffixes to change the words.

smart_____   help_____   use_____

slow _–ly___   wish _–ful___   fear _–less__

love_____   care_____   end_____

❷ Write the words and underline the suffix.

_____   _____   _____

_____   _____   _____

_____   _____   _____

❸ Write words that end with –ly, –ful or –less to complete the sentences.

- Vijay was _____ when he won the prize.   **speech**

- We had a _____ holiday with friends.   **wonder**

- Ann was very _____ when Gran was ill.   **help**

- The blunt knife was _____ for cutting.   **use**

- She was dressed _____ .   **smart**

- The mess was _____ cleared up.   **quick**

Words with soft c

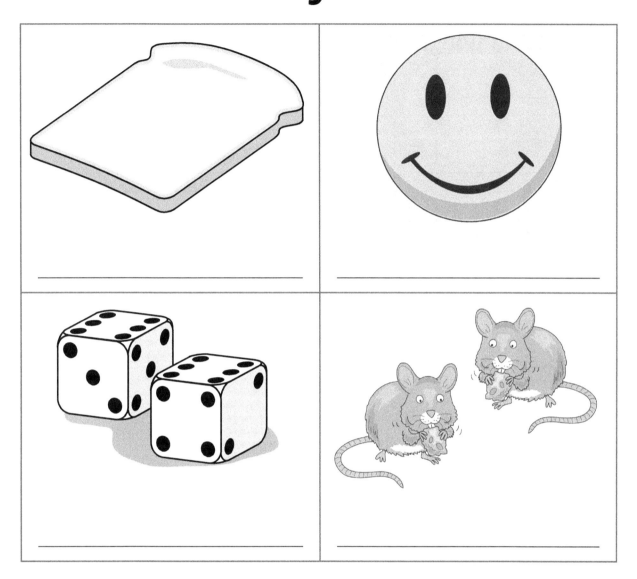

Complete the sentences using the words in the box.

lace	race	rice

- He was very happy when he won the _____ .

- _____ is a good food to eat.

- The dress was trimmed with _____ .

End of unit assessment

❶ Match the beginning of each story sentence with its ending.

Arthur gazed	until their legs felt like jelly.
The more Arthur gazed,	up at the clouds.
Soon he met	at a party.
Soon they arrived	over the fields and back to Flora.
They jumped and danced ...	a hippo.
Off Arthur flew,	the more funny shapes he saw.

❷ Underline the verb in each sentence. List the verbs here.

_____

_____

_____

Speech bubbles

1 Read the speech bubbles.

2 Cut out the speech bubbles.

3 Use the speech bubbles to complete the conversation in your workbook.

Too many sheep.

Not enough sheep.

What do you want?

Can I come in?

I can pay.

Yes.

Good night, and good luck!

We never have any luck.

Question words

Write five questions that the police officer might ask the staff at the sports centre. Try to use a different question word for each one.

1 _____

_____

2 _____

_____

3 _____

_____

4 _____

_____

5 _____

_____

End of unit assessment

1 Write a description of a clown.

Describe the clown using at least four of the words below. Use other interesting words of your own.

_____

_____

_____

_____

_____

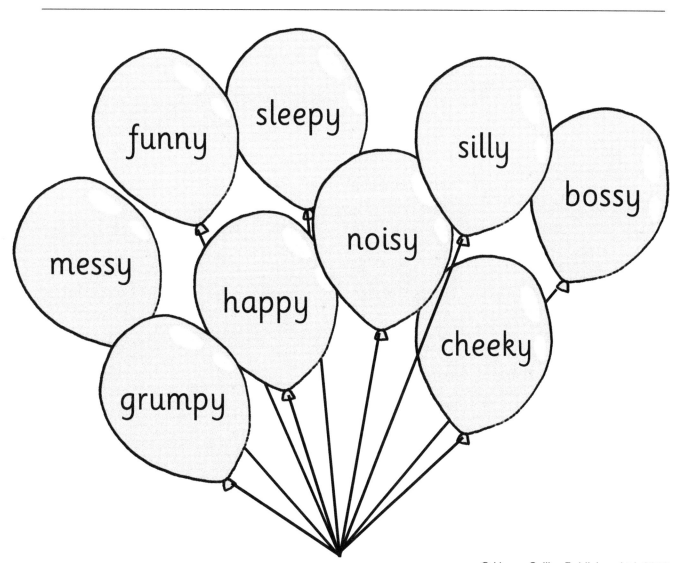

funny

sleepy

silly

bossy

messy

noisy

happy

cheeky

grumpy

Compound words

lady + bird = ladybird

1 Write the word under each picture and then write the compound word.

____ + ____		= ____
____ + ____		= ____
____ + ____		= ____
____ + ____		= ____
____ + ____		= ____
____ + ____		= ____
____ + ____		= ____

End of unit assessment

Tick the box if the sentence is true.

An oil fire can burn like a huge flaming torch.	
Fire helps forests grow.	
Firefighters work as a team.	
Firefighters use jets of water from hosepipes to put out flames.	
Fire fighters use jet skis to put out fires on oil tankers.	
Firefighters put out fires all over the world.	
Fire gives us heat and light.	
Helicopters water-bomb house fires.	

Text acknowledgements

The publishers gratefully acknowledge the permissions granted to reproduce copyright material in the book. Every effort has been made to contact the holders of copyright material, but if any have been inadvertently overlooked, the Publisher will be pleased to make the necessary arrangements at the first opportunity.

HarperCollins*Publishers* Limited; Fraser Ross for an extract and artwork from *Jodle the Juggler* by Vivian French, illustrated by Beccy Blake, text copyright © Vivian French. Joyce Vallar for the adapted poem 'Jason the Juggler', published in *Hector Hedgehog's Big Book of Rhymes*, copyright © Joyce Vallar; HarperCollins*Publishers* Limited; Caroline Sheldon for an extract and artwork from *Worm Looks for Lunch* by Julia Donaldson, illustrated by Martin Remphry, text copyright © Julia Donaldson; HarperCollins*Publishers* Limited; David Higham Associates for *Kind Emma* by Martin Waddell, illustrated by David Roberts, text copyright © Martin Waddell; Robert Charles Howard for the poem 'Dolphin Ballet' published in *Unity Tree*: *Collected Poems by Robert Charles Howard*, 2007, Createspace, copyright © Robert C. Howard; HarperCollins*Publishers*; Lucas Alexander Whitely Agency for *The Dolphin King* by Saviour Pirotta, illustrated by Fausto Bianchi, text copyright © Saviour Pirotta; HarperCollins*Publishers* for *World's Deadliest Creatures* by Anna Claybourne, copyright © Anna Claybourne; HarperCollins*Publishers*; Catchpole Agency for *When Arthur Wouldn't Sleep*, written and illustrated by Joseph Theobald, copyright © Joseph Theobald; HarperCollins*Publishers*; Caroline Sheldon; Juliette Lott for *The Pot of Gold* by Julia Donaldson, illustrated by Sholto Walker, text copyright © Julia Donaldson; HarperCollins*Publishers* for *Fire! Fire!* by Maureen Haselhurst.